"The overwhelming need for validation (us! 'See me, love me, affirm me,' is our on Sundays, even as we send our Chri Whether you're a stage actress or a stay-at-home mom, Lisa Lloyd carries us all along on her journey in the spotlight so that we might learn to purposefully live our lives turning that same beam of light on Jesus. After all, He is the Light of the World . . . and all the world's His stage! Packed full of Scripture truth and resonating examples of biblical characters who lived their unique stories for such a time as this, Chasing Famous inspires readers to offer up their own personal narratives for God's ultimate glory! Inspiring, challenging, and such an important read for each of us living in this digital age that lauds applause on Christian fame."

—WENDY SPEAKE, actress, speaker, and author of *Life Creative: Inspiration for Today's Renaissance Mom* and *Triggers*

"Lisa Lloyd has written a book that relentlessly fixes our eyes on Jesus. She candidly shares her story of finding purpose inside and outside the lights of the stage and film. The struggle she unveils is universal. As you turn these pages, she will ask you the same questions about your life. This book is for you. It will inspire and challenge you."

—TRACY LEVINSON, author of *Unashamed: Candid Conversations About Dating, Love, Nakedness and Faith*

"After a speaking event, I asked two young girls what they dreamed of doing one day. They both said they dreamed of 'being famous.' My heart sank. This desire for fame is an ageless epidemic perpetuated by a deep desire to be valued, needed, and important. Lisa speaks right to the heart of this epidemic in a creative and engaging way through both personal reflection and God's Word. I am so thankful God made it clear to Lisa that this is her purpose . . . to use the story God has written in her life to bring Him fame."

—JENN SPRINKLE, cofounder of The Well Studio

"Lisa Lloyd has written an inspiring story about the twists and turns of life and how God uses all circumstances to show His love and grace. Chasing Famous is perfect for a soul searching study of God's plan for our life and His glory."

—JODIE LAUBENBERG, Texas State Representative, author of landmark pro-life legislation, HB2

"Chasing Famous is a delightfully creative book that reminds us of our true purpose on this earth. In her unique and winsome style, Lisa Lloyd shares her heart and inspires us to live a life that points to God's glory, not our own. This book will help you change your perspective and encourage you to use your gifts and talents in a positive and powerful way to honor God and build His Kingdom."

—KAROL LADD, author of *The Power of a Positive Woman*

"This book is a helping hand to those who are chasing down the wrong path or perhaps are on the right one but have grown weary. Lisa invites you to join along on her adventure with the Lord and reminds you of the sweet life He offers. Regardless of what your present energy is, press on, read this book. It will refuel your tank and remind you of how God intended for this performance we call life to play out."

"I can't remember the last time I felt this excited after reading a book! Lisa is a wicked talented, wise, inspiring girlfriend and Jesus-girl. I'm not an actor, but I can clearly picture myself in every story and easily relate it to my own life. In fact, Chasing Famous reminded me of my passions and how important they are. Moreover, it filled me with motivation to live out my particular calling with zeal for God. This book will positively transform you, and you'll be bubbling over with fresh excitement at all the possibilities ahead of you. I cannot stop thinking about this book. Everyone I know will be getting a copy!"

"In our self-absorbed, consumer-oriented world, we easily forget that God does not exist for us. Rather we exist for Him. Lisa Lloyd invites us into her own life journey and shares her growing desire to make God famous. She is a great storyteller, and her use of Scripture is both accurate and engaging. You will not only appreciate her creativity, you will also relate to her vulnerability and honesty. In Chasing Famous, Lisa inspires us to be more intentional about living our lives and using our gifts to point people to God and His glory."

"The number-one question I am asked on a weekly basis is, 'What am I supposed to be doing with my life?' No matter what season of life a woman is in, there seems to be the question, 'Am I doing what God created me to do?' This book provides a honest look into the answer to these questions and more. I know this book will help women discover who God created them to be and provide a challenge to make Jesus famous!"

"As a Dad who has lost a child, Chasing Famous reminded me to continue to use my story, both the heartache and the healing, to make God famous."

CHASING FAMOUS

Living the Life You've Always Auditioned For

LISA LLOYD

NEW HOPE®
PUBLISHERS
Gospel-Centered. Missions-Driven.

BIRMINGHAM, ALABAMA

New Hope® Publishers
PO Box 12065
Birmingham, AL 35202-2065
NewHopePublishers.com
New Hope Publishers is a division of WMU®.

Library of Congress Cataloging-in-Publication Data
Names: Lloyd, Lisa, 1978- author.
Title: Chasing famous : living the life you've always auditioned for / Lisa
   Lloyd.
Description: Birmingham, AL : New Hope Publishers, 2017.
Identifiers: LCCN 2016052873 (print) | LCCN 2016055166 (ebook) | ISBN
   9781625915177 (permabind) | ISBN 9781596699700 (Ebook)
Subjects: LCSH: Identity (Psychology)--Religious aspects--Christianity. |
   Self-actualization (Psychology)--Religious aspects--Christianity. |
   Vocation--Christianity.
Classification: LCC BV4509.5 .L585 2017 (print) | LCC BV4509.5 (ebook) | DDC
   248.4--dc23
LC record available at https://lccn.loc.gov/2016052873

ISBN-13: 978-1-62591-517-7

N174115 • 0317 • 2.5M1

To the Famous One

CONTENTS

PREFACE

To the Reader,

I can't tell you how excited I am that you're reading this book.

Chasing Famous is about you and for you as you seek to find out why God has you here in the first place. Maybe like me, despite all you have going for you, you still ask these questions, "Why am I here? What does God want me to do with my life? Am I missing anything?" Whether you're a young adult, a stay-at-home mom, the CEO of a company, living paycheck to paycheck, single, married, happy, sad, fulfilled, or longing for more, this book is about your true purpose.

As you open these pages, you'll watch me struggle to find and keep my own purpose. I'll show you all sides of me, even the icky sides. But as you read, I hope you discover that you're not alone when you wrestle with God, and you're not alone as you dance with Him.

I'm an actor. So I couldn't help but title each chapter with a term from "the business" and talk about my experience as an actor throughout the book.

Take notes, and jot down anything the Lord is saying to you. You'll also find questions to consider at the end of each chapter.

As you read I'm praying for God to meet you right where you are and mold your heart to His as He calls you forward on your own adventure to lengthen the fame of His name.

Making God famous with you,

 Lisa

To Markus, my husband and biggest fan: Thank you for listening to me think-out-loud my chapter ideas for hours in the kitchen, on dates, and in text messages. Your wisdom and creativity helped me streamline my thoughts and think outside the proverbial box. You believe in me when I don't believe in myself, and your faith in me pushes me beyond what I think I can do. You are a walking example of a life lived for the fame of God's name. You follow God resolutely, and I will follow you wherever you lead us.

To our boys, "Deuce" and Solomon: I love you, I love you. You are God's gift to your daddy and me. I can't promise I'll be a perfect mom, but I promise I'll do my best to make God famous to you. He has special plans for you. Point everything you do back to Him. May your heart's cry be God's renown and His glory for as long as you live.

To Anne Watson: You are my cheerleader. Everyone needs a friend like you in their corner.

To Arica Thompson: Your friendship gave me great courage as I embarked on this journey. I'll never forget it (Isaiah 45:2–5).

To my talent agents, Suzanne Horne and Gillian DeGennaro: Thank you for your contribution to this book and to my life. I don't acknowledge your tireless work on my behalf enough, but your belief in me gives me confidence as an actor, and I'm grateful.

To Mom: Thank you for your endless wisdom. Thank you for loving me like crazy when I started out on this ride. Your prayers and support enabled this book to happen. I love you, Mom.

To my Glorious God: You have transformed my life. It is my honor to hear from You and write for You—I pray this book brings You all the glorious worship You deserve. May I, and all who read this book, never abandon the chase to make You famous.

SECTION 1:

YOUR STORY FOR THE SPLENDOR OF GOD

When I think about it, it seems a little bananas that God wants to use all of us to show Himself off. I mean, doesn't that seem crazy? But the Bible is clear—God wants to use the story of our lives to radiate His fame. We exist for Him. We've been rescued for Him. He doesn't point His finger at our mistakes and screwups. Rather, He points us to the stage so that we can share with the world how truly glorious He is. Will we bravely accept the role He intends for us to play?

Born for This

Spoken Word

What were you born to do? Who were you created to be?
What's the yearning deep within your very soul?
To be a creator, an inventor, a change maker?
A teacher, a preacher, a justice seeker?

But that's just a dream, right? Even though it may keep
us up at night. So we stay put.

We wait for tomorrow. And we wait for a chance. And we
wait to be called. Only to find out we already have.

But we wait. Like a horse at the starting gate.
We know we should and maybe we could. But we just wait.

Wait to give.
And wait to live.

Do you ever ask yourself, "Why?"
Could it be we've agreed with the father of lies?

Who's told us to be scared,
Scared of what she would say, or he would say,
Scared of what could happen if we stepped out in faith
and trusted the God who's already empowered us to be
who He's created us to be?

We hear that snake say,
"You don't need that life; so here, take a bite. And sit
and wait."
'Cause you know you'll fail.

And you don't have time.

You're too old, you're too young.

You're too fat, you're too dumb.

Maybe if you had a few more dimes, you could change the world.

But now is not your time.

But what if the hero women of the Bible had agreed with these lies?

Said, "Yeah, Satan, you're right. I'll sit and watch the world pass on by."

But they jumped in. All in. And like them, it's time to be brave.

Brave like Ruth, who lost so much, she felt like the walking dead.

But she selflessly journeyed to the land of bread.

Boaz became her kinsman redeemer,

And their family tree changed history.

Brave like Esther who thought her life might be ended.

But she patiently waited to see that scepter extended.

Her trust in God's sovereign plan brought Purim to the entire land.

She had God-given braveness.

And you too were created "for such a time as this."

Brave like Mary, who the Bible says was scared,

Because she was just a no-name from Nazareth and would never have dared to think,

That the Savior of the world could be born to an ordinary girl.

But her obedience delivered eternal life to me and you.

Imagine if your obedience brought that to a few.

See, these women decided they didn't have the time to sit around and wait.

But now was the time to make God's name great.

See, if I allow the enemy to get inside my head it's easy to believe all he's said.

So maybe if we want to change our future we need to change our mind.

Say, "No, Satan, that's a lie. I've got God, and He's on my side."

God's given you and me a special plan to bring fame to His name.

To every nation, woman, child, and man.

And our job is to find out what that plan is and set ourselves free.

So let me ask you again. What were you born to do? Who were you created to be?

And let's join hands, you and me.

Standing side by side, each other's biggest fans.

With God in command.

Let's look to our Savior because for us He took the hit.

I'm done with lies, tell Satan he can kiss it.

So let's live wild, let's live brave,

And may we not miss our divine potential.

Let's get reckless.

'Cause you were born for this.

Written and originally performed by Lisa for the Reckless Women's Conference, Preston Trail Community Church in Frisco, Texas, 2014.

2

The Cast List

. . . .

Cast List: A list of actors chosen by the director to play certain roles in a performance. The performance will be the actor's job until the run of the show is completed.

. . . .

 Your name and renown are the desire of our hearts.

—ISAIAH 26:8 NIV

The everlasting, all-sufficient God is infinitely, unwaveringly, and eternally committed to his great and holy name.
—John Piper

Before email, cast lists were taped to the inside of the theater window, visible from the outside. And if the theater was, let's say, an hour's drive from my home, I'd travel the full 60 minutes to read the sheet of paper that listed who was cast and which role they were cast in. I'd drive home elated or in a mess of tears.

I remember one particular cast list posting my senior year in high school. It was for our spring musical, *Annie Get Your Gun*. My best friend, Cyndi, and I were both up for the role of Calamity Jane, one of two leading female characters. Cyndi could sing. No, she could *say-ng*. She could belt every song they gave her at the audition. I tried to keep up, but my confidence waned dramatically as I heard her sing with ease any song they threw at her. I knew she could sing circles around me, but I dreamily hoped the directors would give me the role anyway. Dismissed from callback, we were told the cast list would be taped to the inside of the high school loading dock windows by 6 p.m.

I arrived at 5:45 just in case. Six came and went. 6:15. 6:30. No cast list. I drove back to those loading dock doors ten times before I saw the 8.5-by-11 white sheet of paper in the window at 10:04 p.m. My anxious heart raced in my chest as I ran up the concrete stairs and to the window. My eyes started at the top of the cast list.

Calamity Jane .... Cyndi Kelley

My heart sank. And at the bottom of the cast list . . .

Dancing Chorus........................... Lisa Jones

I was crushed. I walked past other students who had seen the cast list and looked at me with put-on depressed faces as if to meet me in my sadness. "Are you OK?" they'd ask. I smiled while keeping my game face on and said, "Oh yeah, I'm good, totally good." But I was far from totally good. As soon as my rear end hit the driver's seat of my 1986 Chevy Caprice Classic, my face exploded in tears. I went home and cried on my bed for the rest of the weekend.

Twenty years later, I'm still auditioning. Still hoping to see my name on the cast list.

We're not all actors, but we're all striving to see our names on a "cast list" of some kind. To be selected, wanted, needed. Did I get the part? Do they want me? Or will I have to find my worth elsewhere?

* The Audition That Showed Me My Purpose *

My blouse was ironed, my hair curled, and my heels high. I drove down the highway and reviewed my two lines for the audition, "Honey, there she is. Our new baby." I rehearsed them with different inflections, feelings, and tones, working to get the perfect take on the character. I tried to place myself in the shoes of this new mom, imagining life as her. I had to imagine because my husband, Markus, and I never stood at our children's bassinets in the hospital, *ooohing* and *ahhing*, like this new parent. Probably because our two boys never laid quiet long enough for us to get all goo-goo-gaga over them. Or maybe because I was too tired and too catheterized to stand up and walk over and drool with affection.

I took my hand off the steering wheel and wiped my sweaty palm on my pants. Like any good, disciplined actor preparing for an audition, I did vocal warm-ups and face stretches to calm my nerves and center my focus. But these face gymnastics only intensified the fact I was headed to a place where I could be rejected.

This audition wasn't just about the paycheck, I wanted to be selected. Validated. Needed. I wanted the spotlight. And I knew if I booked the job, I would be.

But only for a moment.

Because once my commercial stops running, my TV episode is over, or my billboard comes down, I'm back to another audition, and the cycle begins again.

A highway sign told me there were only two miles until my exit. A burst of adrenaline zipped through my body and flipped my stomach. I thought about how badly I wanted to be what the director was looking for. I continued to run my lines and took deep breaths to slow my racing heart.

All of the sudden, in the midst of this chaos, I had the opposite thought. A thought that, if embraced and acted on, would make me better and would glorify God. I sensed the Holy Spirit say, "Lisa, I want you to go make Me famous today at this audition. Not yourself."

Come again?

Though I loved God, I seldom thought about Him at an audition, except to throw up a prayer asking for Him to help me book the job. So what was I supposed to do differently? I considered that making God famous and not myself meant I would no longer be up for consideration. Could making God famous mean my goal at this audition would no longer be the elevation of myself but the increase of Him?

I continued to imagine how I might change my habitual, self-centered perspective. Instead of sitting in the lobby cloaked in insecure silence, wondering which of these actors might book the gig over me, I'd engage them in conversation. Instead of pretending to be engaged in conversation with them while I really reviewed lines in my head, I'd listen with my face, my ears, and my heart.

When it came time for me to audition, instead of being preoccupied with using my talents to show my worthiness of the director's acceptance, I'd see my gifts as an offering to God, giving back to Him the talent He gave me.

I took a breath and readjusted my grip on the steering wheel. Now, booking the job was up to Him, not me.

This release of pressure sent a flood of peace that drowned my nervousness.

I parked my car, walked in, and embraced this new approach to my work—make God famous.

Did I get cast in the commercial? Nope. But every time I saw that doting mama on TV, I remembered the audition that brought clarity to why God created me and how He wants to use the talents He's given me—for the elevation of His name and His fame. Not mine.

* Purpose Brings Fulfillment *

I once heard someone say purpose is what gives you fulfillment.

We walk through life searching to be fulfilled. We want success, affirmation, and happiness. God puts these desires within us, but He alone can fulfill them. When we look to people or things for the satisfaction of our purpose, we will continue to seek but will always come up wanting.

Maybe, like me, as you strive to find your purpose, you seek the applause of others. But what if the applause dies out? What if they quit thinking we are so great? We feel purposeless. We wonder, *am I doing life right? Am I on the right track?* And so we strive endlessly to get the "high" back.

Maybe we have it all wrong. What if the measuring stick for our success is not our fame and the applause of others but how well we represent and glorify God?

Before we go any farther, let's get one thing clear. God doesn't need me to make Him famous. He's famous all on His own. But only to creation, me, maybe you, and other Christ followers in the world. The rest of the world doesn't acknowledge Him or recognize His fame. But He desperately wants to be famous to them. And He could do this all on His own—and does so when He chooses—but He wants to use you and me to be His fame bearers. God's often only famous to me—the believer—when I'm in a fleeting moment of worship when He reveals to me just how small I am compared to the awesomeness of who He is. But then, when something or someone else grabs my attention, I'm sucked back in to living life with me center stage.

God could just come down and show His splendor to us, and we would find ourselves as close to the ground as possible, wishing it would swallow us whole at the majesty of His glory. But, He has chosen to use *us*, to radiate His splendor to all the world. Just as He used countless characters in the Bible to show Himself off, it is now our turn to show His brilliance to those who need Him. To your spouse, your kids, the hostess at the restaurant, your boss, the widowed neighbor, the family across the street, the office staff at your kid's school, the barista at Starbucks, the child you sponsor through Compassion International, the pregnant teen at your church, the homeless man you always see on the corner, the single mom, the married mom, the woman at the nail salon . . . how long do we have? *Everybody.* This is why you are here. It's why you're still here.

It's your purpose.

God heralded the reason for our existence so many times in Scripture He could have entitled His Holy Writ, "My Plan for My Fame."

His celebrity is the point of the creation story (Genesis 1:27) and the reason for the Exodus (Exodus 8:10; 9:14–16). The prophets Isaiah and Jeremiah couldn't stop talking about the glory of God (Isaiah 26:8; 61:3; Jeremiah 13:11). Nor could King David (Psalm 106:7–8). Ezekiel's entire theology revolved around God's fame (Ezekiel 20:13–14; 36:20–23). God communicated His desire for His glory to Jesus, whose mission on earth was to show off His Father (John 12:27–28; 15:8; 16:14; 17:1–26). God's enemies even recognized the glory of God (Joshua 2:10–11).

God's passion for His renown is found in the books of Deuteronomy (4:35; 7:6), Psalms (72:19), Romans (11:36), 1 Corinthians (6:19–20; 10:31), 1 Peter (2:9, 12; 4:10), and Revelation (21:23), and that's just getting started.

This is the goal of God—that His name and His celebrity be known throughout the world. The surprise? He desires to use you and me to make it happen (Isaiah 43:7).

Our purpose on this earth has nothing to do with us and everything to do with Him—to live for the fame of God's holy name.

To make *God* famous, I have to step out of the spotlight of *my* life. Set aside myself—my self-reliance, my desire for recognition, my self-promotion. Because all of my selfishness keeps me from mirroring God like He knows I can. I must die to all of me to live out what I'm here to do.

You may be saying, "But who am I to deliver the fame of God? I'm not special or talented. And if you could see inside my soul, you'd find someone who's hardly worthy to be used by God." God doesn't call us based on what we have to offer or what we've done but on what He has to offer *through* us and has done *for* us. And therefore, when I live for the fame of God, He receives more glory. The less there is of you and me, the more there is of Him.

Before Rahab feared God, she was a prostitute (Joshua 2). Before Zacchaeus ate lunch with Jesus, he was a money-loving thief with a Napoleon complex (Luke 19:1–10). Before the demon-possessed man met Jesus, he lived among tombs and cut himself with stones (Mark 5:1–20). Before the Apostle Paul met Jesus, he murdered Christians (Acts 22:4–5, 20). And God changed all of these people. God changes us. God reverses the situation. God doesn't call holy people to come to Him, He calls sinners to come and be holy.

And every one of these people went on to make God famous.

God delights in using our shortcomings and even our former disdain for His name to His glory.

> *The saying is trustworthy and deserving of full acceptance, that Christ Jesus came into the world to save sinners, of whom I am the foremost*. But I received mercy for this reason,* that in me, as the foremost, Jesus Christ might display his perfect patience as an example to those who were to believe in him for eternal life. To the King of the ages, immortal, invisible, the only God, be honor and glory forever and ever. Amen.

—1 TIMOTHY 1:15–17 *(author's emphasis)*

*"first in rank" or "chief" in the Greek

We must push back the lies that tell us we aren't worthy of being used by God for His glory. God uniquely created you with gifts and talents for His eminence. Once we embrace that God has selected us for the show that points all glory to Him, we can lean into our ultimate purpose: the elevation of His name and His fame.

The cast list is up. Your name is at the top. Rehearsals are about to begin . . .

Questions to Consider:

» How have you sought your fame in your own life?

» Up until now, what has been your purpose in life?

» Fill in the blanks:

"Success is when I see _____

_____ ."

"Success is when I hear _____

_____ ."

"I feel fulfilled when _____

_____ ."

» Have you ever thought about making God famous in your home, neighborhood, or work?

» If you were to embrace this idea, how might it change the way you live and function in each of these environments?

» What pressure(s) would it relieve?

» Do you think you might feel more pressure? How?

3

The Audience

Audience: "The assembled listeners at a public event, such as a play, movie, concert, or meeting." These spectators may have paid money to attend the event hoping for personal entertainment, knowledge, growth, or a combination.

{ *For am I now seeking the approval of man, or of God?* }

—GALATIANS 1:10

I heard a story once of a novice actor asking a seasoned one, "Why do we do what we do [as actors]?"

The seasoned actor replied, "You want to know why, dear boy? Do you want to know why?"

And coming nose to nose with his protégé, he whispered loudly, "Look at me! Look at me! Look at me! Look at me! Look at me! Look at me! Look at me! Look at me! Look at me!"

The actor's conviction: actors want an audience, someone to look at them and give them validation.

The chance to perform for an *audience* is why actors audition in the first place. It's not to perform on a stage in front of an empty house or act for a camera that's not rolling. Performers come alive in front of an audience. It's the point of rehearsal. It's why we do what we do. Maybe we want to entertain, advertise, or make people think. Or maybe we just want people to look at us. Whatever the reason, the audience is essential.

Performer or not, everyone needs an audience. If you're a server at a restaurant, you need customers. If you sell computers, you need consumers. If you're a group exercise instructor, you need a class. If you're a dentist, you need patients. If you're a blogger, you need readers. If you're a financial advisor, you need people with money. Without an audience, what would you do?

And because an audience is so vital to our lives, we can quickly turn the gathered spectators into an idol we can't get enough of.

* Applaud Me *

Most days, I struggle to replace myself with God in the center-stage spotlight of my life. Too often I care more for the esteem of man than the fame of my Creator. Stepping off stage and allowing Him to stand in my place can be a daily, sometimes hourly, battle. Maybe it is for you too.

The desire to be affirmed spills into just about any part of my life when my performance is on the line. After speaking at events, I used to want to linger in front of the stage, pretending to check email on my phone, so I could hear the audience's thoughts on my message. I wanted to know if they were challenged, if they would apply the truth I tried to speak into their lives. At least that's what I told myself.

But when I really examined the intentions of my heart, I realized I was more concerned with whether they liked *me*. And I only felt as if I achieved success when they did. Everything about the talk could have been perfect. But their opinion about my performance dictated how I felt about my job. I masked people pleasing, which was at my core, with wanting to know if they were closer to Jesus.

My audience was not an audience of One but an audience of everyone.

When I desire to have others affirm my work more than I desire the affirmation of God, it keeps me center stage of my life and God backstage. And I'm yoked to the approval of man instead of the fame of God.

* Love Me, Need Me, Want Me *

Maybe, like me, you need affirmation to feel valued—at work, at school, as a friend, as a wife, as a mom, with your body, or in your relationships. Perhaps you get a burst of happiness when you get an "attagirl" from your boss, a "you're so giving" from the place where you volunteer, or "your house is beautiful" from a neighbor. But if we make the esteem of man our true north, we'll find ourselves lost at sea when the, "wow, look at you" wears off.

Logically we know if people don't approve of us, it's their fault and not ours. I've impressed this upon my boys when they tell me a kid at school said something mean and made them feel "less than."

"If they don't like you, that's their fault," I say. "They're just missing out on how awesome you are." But somehow I don't apply my own advice to myself. If I'm not accepted by whomever I'm trying to collect acceptance from, I too feel "less than."

When we perform for an audience of everyone, they always want something. We can't simply walk onstage and assume we have their acceptance. Just like a musician at a concert can't step onstage and stand there. She has fans who purchased tickets, and she is expected to perform.

It seems many of our relationships on earth—friendships, our relationship with our boss, maybe, but hopefully not, even our marriages—are the same way. In most of our relationships, we give to get. Unless you're a good friend of mine or a family member, you probably picked up this book not because you wanted to show me love but because you wanted something for yourself. I will only get your applause if you like what I have to say. Otherwise, you'll drop this book at the half-price bookstore or regift it. On the other hand, if this book impacts you, you'll tell people about it. In other words, you'll applaud me.

There's no shame living in an "if you, then I" world, right? It's the way we are wired. Why would I buy something that's not going to benefit me in some way? But unlike people in my life, who only applaud when I perform a certain way, God's heart bursts with affection for me before I break the curtain line. Not because of what I've said or done but because I'm His. He's not waiting for any great performance. I don't have to do anything to receive His love and acceptance. So why do I pursue the applause of someone who wants me to give them something instead of the applause of Someone who just wants me for me? Why do I crave man's applause over God's? Because I'm insecure. I can't stand the idea of someone not approving of me, at least someone whose opinions I value. So I'm going to try to get people to like me so I feel better about myself. And in the process become enslaved to people who only love me for what I can give them.

The Lord desires for us to be confident in Him alone. To be confident in His unconditional love. So much so that we don't need anyone else's applause.

He tells us over and over that we've already been selected. We are:

>> *His children* (Romans 8:14; Galatians 4:6)

>> *Complete in Christ* (Colossians 2:10)

>> *Beautiful* (Psalm 45:11)

>> *Holy and blameless in Christ* (Ephesians 1:4)

>> *Without blemish* (Colossians 1:22 NIV)

>> *New creations* (2 Corinthians 5:17)

>> *Forgiven* (Romans 5:8)

>> *Heaven bound* (1 John 5:13; John 5:24)

❋ Audience of One ❋

In the pursuit of seeking only His applause, I tried something at a recent speaking engagement. For days leading up to the event, I prayed that after I spoke I would listen as God reminded me of His pleasure. When the temptation came to yearn for the "you go, girl" from the audience, I prayed His "whoop-whoop" would be enough. I needed His reminder because I was still locked in the negative habit of craving people's affirmation after I left the stage. To make this easier on me, I would have preferred to walk off stage after my talk and out the back door, not even giving myself the opportunity to hear anyone's feedback. But the event planner might not have appreciated my decision to leave without notice, so I decided to stay.

I arrived at the venue prepared. Like all my talks, I spent time praying through the material, researching commentaries, and combing through Scripture. I deeply desired that the women attending would walk away wanting to make God famous. After I finished the message, I took my seat at a table of women whose stares pinned me to my chair as I sipped a nervous drink of iced tea from a glass that was almost as sweaty as I was.

The recurring thoughts crept into my mind. *What are they thinking? Did they like my talk?* But before the thoughts could reach my heart, the Lord answered my earlier prayers, and I felt His satisfaction and delight. I breathed in His sufficiency and breathed out the need for acceptance. He was finally enough. I knew I could walk through the sea of people, talking with them along the way, and confidently head to my car. If no one said an encouraging thing to me, or even if someone said something discouraging, God was enough. The freedom I felt that day was unlike I'd felt at any other speaking event before that one. As the women encouraged me, I continued to hear the Holy Spirit's affirmation ring louder than theirs.

When we believe in our souls that He has selected us and He is enough, our objective becomes to glorify God for His sake in whatever we do, not to receive the applause of others. And owning the fact that we've already been chosen by God restrains us from seeking our own glory. It keeps us from saying, "Love me. Need me. Want me." It allows us to care more for people—to love, need, and want God.

I don't want to spend my time seeking my own glory but rather the glory of God through me. Can you imagine what it might feel like to have a different response the next time you have the opportunity to crave the applause of others? Can you imagine not just saying but truly owning the statement, "God is enough. I need no one else's affirmation. No one else's applause."

May we, maybe for the first time, see ourselves as God sees us. Accepted. Wanted. Valued. May nothing else even come close to the joy this gives us. May we not get sidetracked from advancing the name of God because we're so concerned about our own elevation. And, as a result, may we lift high the name of Jesus for His great fame and glory.

Questions to Consider:

>> In what areas of your life do you seek the applause of others?

>> How do you feel when you don't live up to others' expectations?

>> Close your eyes. Imagine not doing the work that you currently do for the applause of others but instead working for God alone. Would the pressure change? Would your work change?

>> What are some steps you need to take to make this happen?

>> How would seeking the applause of God alone make Him famous?

>> Will you commit to yourself and to God to seek His applause alone the next time you work?

>> After you've completed the questions above, write down what it felt like to seek only His applause.

Method Acting

Method acting: An acting technique in which an actor aspires to complete the emotional breadth of a role. Actors often fully embody the character on and off screen or stage, never ceasing imitation for the duration of the role. Actors sometimes use their life experiences to identify with the character. These experiences can dramatically shape the character, resulting in what the actor feels is an authentic portrayal of the role.

> *Who is a God like You, who pardons iniquity and passes over the rebellious act of the remnant of His possession? He does not retain His anger forever, because He delights in unchanging love.*
>
> —MICAH 7:18 NASB

At my high school, we young actors took to method acting every time we had a role to play. I watched the seniors do it, so I did it too. In rehearsal and even off stage, we would talk to each other as our character, believing that if we stayed in character at all times, we would deliver a more authentic performance. Before the curtain rose, we would rock back and forth in a corner, moaning as we prepared ourselves to feel the pain our sorrowful character needed to feel on stage. Or if the character was not so melancholy, we'd skip and sing to produce a more cheerful performance.

I no longer use method acting, but many well-known actors do. While Dustin Hoffman was filming *Marathon Man*, he once stayed awake for three days to add to the believability of his character. When his costar, Sir Laurence Olivier, discovered this, he said to Hoffman, "My dear boy, why don't you try acting?"

On the television show, *Inside the Actor's Studio*, Hoffman told host James Lipton he was going through a painful divorce during the filming of *Marathon Man*. On top of the lack of sleep, his divorce fueled his emotions, which allowed him to deliver a realistic portrayal of the depth of pain the character felt.

Like method actors, our own life experiences dramatically shape us, resulting in the character we are today. Those experiences ground us and remind us of who we were before Christ and who we are now.

One experience, unlike any other, changed me forever and influenced my life and ministry.

* My Character *

I sat on the bed in the master bedroom watching TV as my mom and her good friend talked in the living room. Most six year old's parents might have turned on Mickey Mouse or Tom and Jerry, but my mom flipped to *The 700 Club*—a Christian news program featuring live guests and daily news. At that particular hour, I was watching a kid-friendly program with talking puppets and singing dogs. I sang along and listened to the stories the puppets and puppies were telling about Jesus and heaven. The talking wonders asked their captivated young audience through the TV screen, "Do you want to know that when you die you will go to heaven?"

I remember thinking, *Yes!*

I prayed a prayer along with those crazy animals, and I confessed with my mouth, "Jesus is Lord," and I believed in my heart God raised Him from the dead. And I was saved (Romans 10:9–10).

But as I grew older I replaced the guiding voice of the Holy Spirit with the voice of peers, particularly young boys. And like too many 15-year-old girls entranced by the desire to be "loved," I gave up my virginity to the first boyfriend who asked.

By the time I was 18, I was pregnant. And scared to death.

I knew I had three options: to carry and parent, to create an adoption plan, or to abort. As a Christian, I knew the only choice was to have the baby. But as a teen in a crisis pregnancy, the only viable choice was abortion. At least that's what I convinced myself. I was more terrified of what others would think of my hypocritical self and of the "end of my life" becoming a teen parent than the safety of this baby. The Holy Spirit wouldn't allow me to believe that this pregnancy was a blob of tissue. In the back of my mind, I knew what grew within me was a precious child who deserved life. And I knew I was choosing to end his or her opportunity. But I didn't allow myself to feel these emotions for fear of connecting my soul to their's. So I walked as quickly as I could to the nearest exit.

* The Exit Door *

A nurse from the abortion clinic called me the day before my appointment. She told me to expect protesters in front of the building; I would need to enter through the back. I pulled up to the clinic and saw the scene described to me on the phone—people with signs pacing in front of the clinic's door. I drove past them in my mom's minivan—a Christian icthus fish glued to the bumper. I can still hear the loose gravel of the parking lot under its tires. I stepped out of the van and walked toward the nurse waiting for me at the back door. Little did I know, a protester saw me drive in and came to the high brick wall framing the parking lot. He had seen the fish on the van's bumper, which he took as permission to remind me of Who loved me. Though I couldn't see him, I heard his desperate voice pleading with me, "Please don't do this! Jesus loves you so much! I saw the fish on the back of your car, and God loves your baby! Please let us help you, we can help you, but please don't do this!" His words became to me the Holy Spirit Himself leaping out of my chest, kneeling before me, and begging me with audible words.

A different exit door and a way out of this chaos and into freedom. But I didn't walk through.

I was soon lying on the table for my sonogram. The sonographer was careful to keep the screen pointed away from me.

"You're too early," she said.

"What?"

"You have to be between seven and nine weeks for an abortion, and you're not far enough along yet."

In 1996, the year I laid on that table, neither the morning-after pill—to purge a possible pregnancy the morning after sex—or RU-486—the series of pills women take for abortions between one and seven weeks of pregnancy—had been discovered yet. Surgical abortion was the only option. And my baby wasn't developed enough to undergo the end of his or her life.

Unable to have an abortion that day, I left. Another opportunity to confront my sin and find freedom. Another exit door.

I wish I could say I opened this door, but I didn't. I wish I could say my two boys have a 19-year-old half sister. But they don't. At least not here on earth.

Two months later I sat on my bed talking with a friend on the phone. She had the opposite relationship with God that I had: resolute and strong—like an army tank resistant to the bullets of temptation. For the last several years, she lovingly asked me why I walked away from God like I did. She cast a vision of the plans God had for me but couldn't implement if I wouldn't let Him. Each time, I shrugged her off and walked away.

But this night was different. It was the first time she'd asked me these questions since the abortion. I felt raw and vulnerable. She reminded me of the unconditional love of Jesus, and my heart softened. For the first time, I saw the gravity of my sin, and I wanted to change. It was like scales fell from my eyes revealing color instead of the fuzzy gray I'd learned to call normal.

As I rose out of the fog, I saw my life below me and was distraught as I reviewed the previous years with new eyes. I expressed my anguish to God at the devastation I'd taken Him through. But He silenced my deep distress with His response. It was almost as if He said, "Oh, Lisa, there's nothing you could ever do that would make Me not love you."

I quickly reminded Him of my years of lying, promiscuity, and murder.

But His voice was louder, "All the more amazing, then is My grace. Lisa, I'm crazy about you. And I will use you and your sin for My great glory and fame. But you will have to walk away from this life. You're going to have to turn 180 degrees in the opposite direction and follow Me. It won't be easy. But I promise, I'll make it worth it."

And so I did. And He did. And I've never been the same.

{ *Therefore, if anyone is in Christ, he is a new creation. The old has passed away; behold, the new has come.* }

—2 CORINTHIANS 5:17

＊ A New Creation ＊

After I graduated high school, I attended Southern Methodist University as a theater major. I joined Campus Crusade for Christ and was discipled by a Crusade staff member throughout my four years there. She taught me how to read my Bible, pray, memorize Scripture, and disciple other women.

I raised my standards of dating and thought dating guys who went to church was a good place to start. When I realized churchgoing guys didn't necessarily love Jesus, I raised my standards again and asked God to bring me relationships that furthered my relationship with Him and brought Him glory. I also prayed that the Lord would bring me a husband one day who loved Him more than he loved me. I knew that if my husband loved Jesus more than me, he would love me well because his authority would not be himself or his desires but Jesus. I wanted to be the kind of woman this kind of guy would be attracted to. So I worked on knowing God well and becoming the woman He knew I could be.

And God answered my prayers.

I met my husband while performing in a theater production in downtown Dallas. Aside from being incredibly good looking, I noticed how uniquely nice he was. People were drawn to him. As we spent time together, I learned he wasn't just a guy who said he went to church and said he read his Bible. Jesus was everything to him. Ten months later he proposed.

When I told him about my past, he enveloped me in his arms and rocked me back and forth and praised the Lord saying, "I cannot believe what Jesus has done through you. I don't even see a glimpse of the Lisa of your past. You are transformed! God is amazing!"

The Chiseling Hand of God

When we had been married five years, and ten years after my abortion, I went through postabortion group counseling. I was very reluctant because I didn't think I needed counseling. I knew I'd been forgiven —what more was there to learn? But there was so much more. In those two months of counseling, every day I learned something new that the Lord was trying to show me. He helped me deal with buried emotions of grief and chiseled away the hardened clay of shame and guilt. He showed me His passion for the unborn and unheard and His feverish anger against abortion. I saw the gravity of my sin in light of Holy God and yet the radical grace and love of Jesus in spite of it. During this time, God impressed upon my heart the full personhood of my unborn child, and I realized that her name is Christine.

At the end of those two months, each of the women in the counseling group had a chance to release their children into the arms of Jesus. When Christine's name was called, I walked to the table with a white rose in hand, picked up her certificate of life and replaced it with the rose. I sat down next to my husband, closed my eyes, and cried. These weren't tears of grief but gratitude at the goodness of our great God.

And then, though my eyes were closed, I saw something in my mind's eye that I will never forget. A young girl with long, dark brown hair much like mine. She wore a white dress, was barefoot, and stood with her back to me. Though I couldn't see her face, I knew her— Christine. Joy and light radiated from her body. She was alive, and she was complete. I recognized someone else with her. It was Jesus. I saw the profile of His face as He extended His hand to her and she placed her little hand in His. Together, He walked and she skipped away from me. And they disappeared. And I sensed sweet Jesus whisper to me, "I've got her, Lisa. I've got her."

And He has since said to me, "Now go. And make Me famous."

God is in the business of using our past experiences to influence the "character" we are today.

Maybe you have experienced the redemption of Jesus. Or maybe you haven't yet. Either way, Jesus died in your place and mine, saving us, not for us ultimately, but for His great glory. The endgame of His Cross was the elevation of His fame. So that when we talk about "our character" before we knew God and who we are now with God, our story would make Him famous.

The prophet Isaiah foretells the saving power of Jesus Christ in Isaiah 61:

The Spirit of the Sovereign LORD is on me, because the LORD has anointed me to proclaim good news to the poor. He has sent me to bind up the brokenhearted, to proclaim freedom for the captives and release from darkness for the prisoners, to proclaim the year of the LORD's favor and the day of vengeance of our God, to comfort all who mourn, and provide for those who grieve in Zion—to bestow on them a crown of beauty instead of ashes, the oil of joy instead of mourning, and a garment of praise instead of a spirit of despair. They will be called oaks of righteousness, a planting of the LORD for the display of his splendor.

—ISAIAH 61:1–3 NIV *(author's emphasis)*

* A Display of His Splendor *

You and I were saved from the oppression of sin and Satan so our life change would be an obvious display of the splendor of God and His glory.

{ *In him we have obtained an inheritance . . . so that we who were the first to hope in Christ might be to the praise of his glory. In him you also, when you heard the word of truth, the gospel of your salvation, and believed in him, were sealed with the promised Holy Spirit, who is the guarantee of our inheritance until we acquire possession of it, to the praise of his glory.* }

—EPHESIANS 1:11–14 *(author's emphasis)*

About the above passage, the *English Standard Version* study notes in my Bible say, "God's ultimate purpose is not redemption as such but the *praise* of His glorious name through redemption."

God's desire is not just your salvation but that He could be made famous and known because of it.

Before we can begin the battle to make God famous, we must know how the enemy operates.

Questions to Consider:

» Which experience or experiences in your life have made you into who you are today?

» Do you find that, like a "method actor," you recall those experiences to ground you and, as you do, those experiences influence you today?

» What has God saved you from?

» How does this make you feel?

» How could He possibly use His story through you for His glory and fame?

» Are you allowing Him to do this?

» If you didn't stand in His way, imagine how God could make His Name known through your story of His salvation. Write down what that could possibly look like.

5

Projection

My sin—oh, the bliss of this glorious thought!

My sin, not in part but the whole,

Is nailed to the Cross, and I bear it no more,

Praise the Lord, praise the Lord, oh my soul!

—H. Spafford, "It is Well With My Soul"

And I heard the voice of the Lord saying, "Whom shall I send, and who will go for us?" Then I said, "Here I am! Send me."

—ISAIAH 6:8

I performed in the outdoor show, *Texas*, in Palo Duro Canyon for two summers when I was in college. The canyon wall served as the backdrop of the stage, and it was breathtaking. The amphitheater was also ginormous. Nearly 2,000 seats took up the house, and acting in this space sometimes felt as if I were performing in a sports stadium. Though the size of the house was enormous, we didn't have microphones. Why? I have no idea. Thankfully, the show now uses mics. But when I performed, projection was a must. Projection doesn't mean, "Sing out, Louise," as Momma Rose says in the musical *Gypsy*; it is a technique in which actors activate the diaphragm muscle to support their sound. This support enables their voices to hit the back wall of the theater so the audience can hear them. The other option is for the actor to use their throat, and eventually they will lose their voice. Projection was imperative in the large outdoor amphitheater during the show, which ran six nights a week for three months.

In the canyon, there were many elements that absorbed our sound—the audience members, the wind, and even the downpour of rain. We had to push through these enemies to communicate if we wanted to be heard.

God asks redeemed people, like actors, to project His fame to the back wall and to do it over and over and over again so the listening audience can hear. But there is a great enemy to our communicating God's fame—Satan himself. And if we're not paying attention and using our support (namely, depending on God), Satan will absorb our sound and silence us.

The enemy's endgame is the exact opposite of God's, and we are guaranteed to battle Satan. His goal is to keep our life experiences from shaping our character. He will tell us lies, and we will be extremely tempted to believe him and stay silent about our stories. Fear, embarrassment, and shame will draw us to keep our lips closed and the door to our past locked.

The enemy silenced my projection for years.

* Closet Doors and Courtrooms *

Throughout college, I kept my abortion a secret. I never told my roommate or the woman who discipled me. Though I embraced the Cross and knew I was forgiven, I worried about what people would think of me and that any hypocrisy they assumed of me would defame the name of God. So I stayed silent.

I kept my dark past behind a locked closet door. Hidden and quiet, my story was safe in the shadows. And this is where I believed it belonged. I listened to the lies, and lies kept me imprisoned. I lived forgiven but not free.

Many of us might say the same about ourselves even now. Past sins tie us down, burdens imprison us, and we feel trapped and bound by the thoughts that plague our heads and consume our hearts.

But when Jesus died for us, He didn't die for us to stay in prison but to live free. I love how Colossians describes this.

> *[God] having forgiven you all trespasses; blotting out the handwriting of ordinances that was against us, which was contrary to us, and took it out of the way, nailing it to his cross; and having spoiled principalities and powers, he made a shew of them openly, triumphing over them in it.*

—COLOSSIANS 2:13–15 KJV

The word translated "handwriting of ordinances" is translated from the Greek word *cheirographon*. It was used to refer to the written evidence of a person's guilt, for which they must pay a penalty. It was the written record of a person's crimes—the laws he or she had broken and the penalty owed for law breaking. "Out of the way" is translated, "out of the middle." In ancient times the accuser would present the *cheirographon* from the "middle" of the courtroom.

Paul is describing, here, an allegorical heavenly courtroom, before Christ cancelled our debts on the Cross. God is the presiding Judge. In this scenario, you have been arrested and brought into His courtroom.

The prosecuting attorney is Satan, who has brought you before the Judge and wants to silence any testimony (projection) you could have about the redemption of God. In his hands Satan holds a *cheirographon*, and in his handwriting is written every sin you have ever committed. The information on this document is not based on hearsay or unfounded suspicions. It is recognized by the court as a legal and legitimate document.

Satan presents the *cheirographon* to the Judge.

But you have an Advocate with you in the courtroom of God. "And if anyone does sin, we have an advocate with the Father, Jesus Christ the righteous" (1 John 2:1). Your Advocate admits that the information on the *cheirographon* is true. You have indeed committed all these crimes, and you do indeed deserve the death penalty and to spend your eternal life apart from God.

However, your Advocate says, the penalty for all your crimes has already been fully paid on the Cross.

Because of this, the Judge tells Satan that his *cheirographon* is inadmissible evidence in the heavenly courtroom. Therefore the *cheirographon* that "was against us, which was contrary to us," is taken out of the way (Colossians 2:14 KJV). It is removed from the middle of the courtroom occupied by the accuser. Then it is "nail[ed] to His cross" like a banner, proclaiming the Messiah's triumph over sin on our behalf.

This image of our sins being nailed to a cross is an allusion to Bible times. Historically, when a person was crucified, a notice declaring the crime they committed was fastened over their head. You may remember the notice Rome nailed above Jesus' head when they crucified Him—the "sin" of proclaiming to be King of the Jews (John 19:19–20).

Our sins were nailed to Jesus' Cross as if He had committed the sins, and He took our penalty.

By paying the penalty for our sins, Jesus ruined the adversary's plans to condemn us with the *cheirographon*. That is why the very next verse says, "And having spoiled principalities and powers, he made a shew of them openly, triumphing over them in it" (Colossians 2:15 KJV). Satan was stripped of his power to now accuse us before God.

The Judge says to you, "There's nothing you have to do, nothing you have to pay. You're free to go. You're free."

I once heard a pastor say that Jesus' death in your place was not only meant to pay for the punishment of your sin so that you could be forgiven but also to deliver you from the power of sin so that you could live for Him.

Amen and amen.

Released but Still Bound

Here's what often happens to us. Forgiven and set free by God, we leave the courthouse. And while Satan has no power to accuse us before God, he follows us down the courthouse steps and whispers in our ear that we are not free and victorious in Christ. He tells us lies about ourselves and lies about God.

>> *"Aren't you ashamed of your past screwups? You are still a total failure."*

>> *"God is so disappointed in you. Wouldn't you be?"*

>> *"Don't tell anyone about what God has done through you. You'll be seen as such a hypocrite."*

>> *"You don't deserve God's forgiveness."*

>> *"God didn't really forgive you completely. The pain you're going through now is a result of the sin of your past."*

And we agree with Satan about these lies and about ourselves. We return to the courthouse, put our handcuffs back on, and sit inside our jail cell. Even though the door is wide open for us to leave. And so we live forgiven but not free. Because Satan lies, and we believe him.

And he wins. He's been doing it since the Garden of Eden, and he won't stop. He's been watching humanity for a long time and knows that as long as you're in prison and focused on you and what a screwup you are, you can't be out projecting God's redemption and making Him famous—which is ultimately why Jesus saved you from sitting in jail in the first place.

* Free at Last *

It wasn't until I said no to Satan and started talking about who I used to be that I experienced freedom. When I stopped believing the lie, I took off my chains and opened the door to my past so that the light of Jesus could shine on it. As I share my story of coming from bondage to freedom, people find bravery to share their stories too. And Satan is defeated. When we stop believing the lie, freedom comes, and Satan loses his grip on us.

The only antidote to believing lies and being truly free is to replace the lies with truth. To say, "No, I'm not believing that lie." To fight Satan with the sword of truth, which is the Word of God (Ephesians 6:17).

To believe that we are truly forgiven.

> *I, I am he who blots out your transgressions for my own sake,*
> *and I will not remember your sins.*
>
> —ISAIAH 43:25

> *For I will be merciful toward their iniquities, and I will*
> *remember their sins no more.*
>
> —HEBREWS 8:12

> *As far as the east is from the west, so far does he remove*
> *our transgressions from us.*
>
> —PSALM 103:12

And to tell our story.

> *"Go home to your friends and tell them how much the Lord*
> *has done for you, and how he has had mercy on you." And he*
> *went away and began to proclaim in the Decapolis how much*
> *Jesus had done for him, and everyone marveled.*
>
> —MARK 5:19–20

We might think that telling our story will result in people thinking less of us—which is really just a desire to make ourselves famous in the eyes of others. But in actuality, telling our stories glorifies God as people see that only He could transform our lives. They watch His grace unfold through us.

Maybe you've never shared your story, and you're scared to death to do so. Maybe you've never told your husband, your kids, your parents, your friends. Maybe you believe, as I used to, that if people hear your story, they will think less of you and a lot less of God.

But when I talk about my past people never say, "What were you thinking? Sex? Abortion? How could you? What a hypocrite!" Instead their response is the opposite, "How amazing is God?" They stand with mouths agape in awe of Him. They rejoice at His amazing redemption and transformation of the woman in front of them. While I used to think that people would focus their attention on my bad choices if I told them the truth, I have found that I am not even discussed. Only God and how awesome He is. And He is made famous.

I believe the same will be true for you—through God's proclamation of "liberty to the captives, and the opening of the prison to those who are bound" (Isaiah 61:1) our stories of redemption will bring Him great glory. To believe otherwise is to believe a lie. God is glorified when we share our stories. It takes guts and bravery. But it makes Him famous.

May we refuse to stay imprisoned any longer. May we stop listening to the enemy who wants us to stay silent. Let's leave the prison walls and run to the stage to project His fame and His great name. And as a result, may those who might have never believed God could forgive them hear us loud and clear and risk trusting Jesus. The call to make God famous through the telling of our stories is not just for you but for all who hear.

Let's live forgiven and set free.

Questions to Consider:

>> Have you ever considered the enemy's fury at God's salvation of you? Do you think Satan will stop at anything to keep you from making God famous?

>> Who knows the full story of who you were before Christ and who you are after?

>> What if you were to tell your story the next time you had the opportunity?

>> What would that feel like? Would you be scared or empowered?

>> Do you think people could be set free as they hear your story?

>> How might the telling of your story make God famous?

>> How might the silence of your story defame Him?

>> Can you think of anyone who needs to know? Your kids? Your spouse? A friend?

6

Encore

Encore: A repeated or additional performance at the end of a concert, as called for by an audience.

The message of biblical Christianity is not, "God loves me, period" as if we were the object of our own faith. The message of biblical Christianity is "God loves me so that I might make Him—His ways, His salvation, His glory, and His greatness—known among all nations." Now God is the object of our faith and Christianity centers around Him. We are not the end of the Gospel; God is.

—David Platt, *Radical*

You've probably been to a theater production where, by the applause of the audience, the cast is asked to sing one last time before the curtain comes down. And you probably wouldn't be surprised to learn that the cast is always prepared for this. In many musicals, a song from the show is slated to be sung after the bows. It's written into the score. After the bows in the curtain call, the cast stands together at the front of the stage, and they sing one of the most well-loved tunes, usually upbeat, to leave a happy memory in the audience's minds. In the theater world, this song is called the encore.

One of the most moving encores I've ever seen was in *Les Misérables: The Dream Cast in Concert*. It is a concert version of the musical and was produced to celebrate its tenth anniversary. It was filmed in October 1995 at the Royal Albert Hall in London and released on DVD (and VHS, if you can remember what that is!) in 1998. At the end of the show, the cast stood at the front of the stage and sang their final song, "Do You Hear the People Sing?" The audience erupted with applause. The cast took their well-deserved bows, and then something happened I never expected. Seventeen Jean Valjeans, the lead male character in *Les Misérables*, from all over the world came through the center of the audience, each carrying a flag representing their home country in which they played the role. Then, all the Valjeans lined the front of the stage and sang a line in their own language from, "Do You Hear the People Sing?" This led into the entire cast and choir of more than 200 members closing with the song "One Day More." The audience leapt to its feet, and the applause and cheers were deafening. The theatergoers were moved to tears as this cast gave a tireless, passionate delivery of the production.

✱ The Church's Encore ✱

I was moved to tears as well, not only because the performances were so well conveyed and sung but because it was a picture of how I believe God desires that we, the church, stand in unison, proclaiming His fame to a captivated audience desperately in need of our message.

The church is called to stand as a nation of sinners, proclaiming our need for Jesus, and singing about the truth of our God. We are supposed to fight the battle for the fame of God not only as individuals but as a united front.

> *But you are a chosen race, a royal priesthood,* a holy nation, *a people for his own possession, that you may* proclaim the excellencies of Him *who called you out of darkness into his marvelous light.*
>
> —1 PETER 2:9 *(author's emphasis)*

The world needs to see, through the vocal body of Christ, that its sin is no match for the love of God. This has been God's method of operation for all time—God doesn't just tell us about His love, He shows us.

* Hosea and Gomer *

Through his relationship with his wife, Gomer, Hosea was called by God to visibly represent God's forgiving arms. Just like Israel sinned and went after other "lovers" instead of God, Gomer sinned against Hosea and went after other lovers instead of seeing Hosea as the one who loved her the most.

When the LORD first spoke through Hosea, the LORD said to Hosea, "Go, take to yourself a wife of whoredom and have children of whoredom, for the land commits great whoredom by forsaking the LORD."

—HOSEA 1:2

Essentially God said to Hosea (author's paraphrase), "I've been pursuing Israel for years, but they don't turn back to me. I set them apart as a people to make Me famous on this earth. We've made a covenant together that they will be My people, and I will be their God. And so I've provided food and water and clothing, rescued them from war, famine, slavery, and extinction. But they are unfaithful to Me. They have seen the gods of others and have taken those gods to be their own. They have inappropriate relationships with cult prostitutes in order to get the gods to rain on their land and produce crops. They worshipped the Baals and the Ashtaroth*. They cut themselves and sacrifice their own children to get their gods to notice them. They think this will be the way to get what they want and need, when I am the only way. So I need you, their leader, to show them their sin. They need a mirror. Show them that they commit adultery against me. They have been unfaithful, over and over again, despite My relentless love for them. If only they would turn back to Me, I could show them that I love them no matter what. So go, take for yourself the kind of wife who will do to you what Israel does to Me."

* *

Pronounced: ash·tä·rōth'

So Hosea "took Gomer" (Hosea 1:3), like God took us, and he loved her with the unreserved love of God.

For this metaphor to work, as much as was humanly possible,

Hosea loved Gomer like God loved Israel. The biggest tragedy of it all—he loved her deeply, and she still went off to other lovers.

She wasn't immediately unfaithful to him when they got married. "She conceived and bore him a son" (Hosea 1:3). Notice that she bears *him* a son.

But infidelity crept in. Watch the details of the description of the birth of the next two children. "She conceived again and bore a daughter. And the LORD said to him, 'Call her name No Mercy' . . . When she had weaned No Mercy, she conceived and bore a son. And the LORD said, 'Call his name Not My People'" (Hosea 1:6, 8–9).

She goes from bearing *him* a son to bearing *a* daughter and then another son. And the names of the children also give away that the second and third children are not Hosea's, "No Mercy" and "Not My People."

Things only get worse. Just as Israel attributed God's generosity to them as gifts from Baal, Gomer believes that her lovers meet her needs instead of acknowledging Hosea as her provider.

> *For she said, "I will go after my lovers, who give me my bread*
> *and my water, my wool and my flax, my oil and my drink." . . .*
> *And she did not know that it was I who gave her the grain,*
> *the wine, and the oil, and who lavished on her silver and gold,*
> *which they used for Baal.*
>
> —HOSEA 2:5, 8

Commentator and pastor David Guzik suggests that it was as if Hosea goes to the home where Gomer lives in poverty with her adulterous lover. He knocks on the door, with groceries and money in hand. A man comes to the door, and Hosea asks, "Are you the man living with Gomer? . . . I'm Hosea, her husband. I've brought these groceries and money so she can be provided for."

I imagine the lover snatching the groceries and money out of his hand and slamming the door so he and Gomer could eat Hosea's food that night, laughing at her foolish husband.

Guzik continues, "But this is exactly how the Lord loves us—lavishing blessing on us even when we are worshipping idols, providing us with blessings we waste on other gods."

At this point, any man might be inclined to leave a wife who seems to care nothing for him and laughs in the face of his goodness. But the Lord's love is relentless, and God asks Hosea to again mirror God's love for His people to Gomer. God knew Hosea's deep love for her would cause him to pursue her regardless of the sins against him.

> And the LORD said to me, "Go again, love a woman [Gomer] who is loved by another man and is an adulteress, even as the LORD loves the children of Israel, though they turn to other gods and love cakes of raisins."
>
> —HOSEA 3:1

Through the marriage of Hosea and Gomer, God wants to show His fame and how unending His love is for us, we who rebel against His love.

Hosea 3:2 reveals that Gomer ended up in a place of destitution—where she had nothing and was forced into prostitution. Maybe she'd been beaten by her adulterous lovers, kicked out into the night, and was homeless. Perhaps in order to eat and feed her children, she had to sell her body to anyone who would pay for it.

My imagination creates the scene almost as if from a movie. Gomer stands on a table, naked and dirty, forced to turn in a circle for all the men to see. What complete humiliation. Her choices have landed her here, but the man who loves her regardless of her actions is standing in the crowd.

> So I bought her for fifteen shekels of silver and a homer and a lethech* of barley.
>
> —HOSEA 3:2

Pronounced: le'-thek

Hosea buys back his wife. He redeems her. And he reminds Gomer of his merciful love. "And I said to her, 'You must dwell as mine for many days. You shall not play the whore, or belong to another man; so will I also be to you'" (Hosea 3:3).

David Guzik comments, "Hosea didn't really need to 'buy' his own wife, to hire her as a prostitute. She was his wife! But as a display of love and commitment, he goes the 'extra mile,' beyond what is expected or even reasonable. . . . The point of paying Gomer wasn't just to get her to give up her trade as a prostitute. It was to bring her into relationship with Hosea, her husband."

God provided Hosea as a mirror to Israel to show His unreserved love for them despite their rebellion to go after other lovers. And 700 years later, He sent Jesus to do the same with the Cross and buy us off the table. What a God!

* Called to the Stage *

Now we, as the body of this Christ, have been passed the mic. We get to stand on a stage and proclaim the goodness of God. But like Hosea, we must go one level deeper. We too are to love unconditionally and show everyone His compassion—without judgment. With open arms we are to show God's mercy as the mirror to the world.

To do this, our response to sin must be like Hosea's—without judgment and saturated with unconditional love. With the recognition that no one is better than anyone else, and understanding we all deserve to live eternity separated from Almighty God.

But Jesus.

Jesus provided the only way for us to get back into a right position with God—where we could actually stand before Him without immediate death as a result of our unholiness in the presence of His own holiness. None of us are worthy, but Jesus makes us so.

This is good news to all but especially to those in the crisis of sin, who, like Gomer, have yet to come to know God. To know that God will love you no matter what and that the people of God feel the same.

So why don't we see nonbelieving and even believing sinners running to the body of Christ in droves? Why don't we hear, "Encore! Encore!" at the end of our production that heralds His fame? I believe it's because those in the crisis of sin oftentimes see the body of Christ, the big "C" church, not as forgiving and loving unconditionally but as judgmental, loving only when sin is not present. Or at least not visible.

This is so tragic to me because so many people in the church respond with open arms and an abundance of grace. Sadly, just a few judgmental responses of some believers can be assumed as the heartbeat of all believers.

* Why Planned Parenthood Works *

When I found out I was pregnant, I was terrified for any believer to find out I was pregnant. Part of this was my own fault. I had spent years lying to everyone, and they believed I was the good girl I was letting on to be. But I also heard people in the church bad-mouthing the sins of others, when I knew no one was perfect.

As I grew up, the issue of teen pregnancy was a foreign topic of conversation with the church. Any talk around it was often accompanied by gasps of shock and disappointment. Teen pregnancy was spoken of with pointed fingers, disgust, and gossip masked by a "prayer request."

Likewise, people in similarly derailing situations go to those (who sadly are most often not the body of Christ) who will "safely" hear their pain regarding what they're going through.

Because Planned Parenthood was talking about sex and options for an unwanted pregnancy, they seemed to be a safe haven for me. I believed I could talk to them about my crisis and not be judged. Because of what they advertised, I believed I would get answers and help.

But don't we as the church advertise the absolute love of Jesus? Safety, "no perfect people allowed," and grace? Or do we overpromise and underdeliver?

I went to Planned Parenthood, and I was right.

I was ushered into a comfortable room where my counselor asked me what brought me into the clinic that day. I told her I was pregnant and didn't think I wanted to keep the baby. She told me her own story of teen pregnancy and abortion. She listened to my fears, wiped my tears, and offered me a cup of water . . . and an abortion brochure.

When people are in a crisis situation, I don't want them running to places like Planned Parenthood. I want them running to us, the church. Don't you? We can do this. And for the sake of those seeking the answer to their pain in everything but God, we must do this.

* The Call to the Church to Make God Famous *

The body of Christ offers hope and freedom to any problem. We can't promise the consequences will disappear, and we can't give people a Band-Aid for their problem. But we do offer the Healer to any hurt and the Antidote to any ailment. We offer the unrestricted and unequivocal love of Jesus.

How will people know what God is like if we don't mirror Him to them? If we don't stand on stage and proclaim Him?

We must become people who don't whisper about the sins of others that we see walking down the halls at church. We must refuse to make judgmental comments in front of our kids about people we see on the news. We must stop seeing ourselves as better than anyone else. Instead we must own that we are all sinners standing before a sinless, holy God. And that perspective should make us grateful and keep us humble. Who are we to cast a stone?

This is very difficult for me to do. It's easier for me to think badly about someone than to have compassion on them. If I think negative thoughts about them, then their problem doesn't require anything of me—*they* need to do the work. But compassion? That gets me involved. Now I'm investing my heart, my time, my resources. And that can get messy. But that's what Christians do.

So how do we become a church, a body, that makes God famous?

First, we must recognize that we are no better than the worst criminal in the eyes of God. This comes through asking God to reset our minds and see others as He does. We know we are on the right track when we look at other sinners and ache for their redemption instead of punishment for their crime.

Second, we must talk about our *own* sin—not gossip about the sins of others. As a result, freedom will be found, and people will be set free.

* Vulnerability Breeds Vulnerability *

Have you ever noticed, maybe in a small group or on social media, when one person shares his or her story, others feel comfortable to share theirs as well? That's because vulnerability breeds vulnerability. The reason organizations like Planned Parenthood work is because they are talking about what the church seems too scared to discuss. We must be bold and brave to talk about the hard topics, to share our stories of sin and redemption regardless of what others may think. Once we start sharing, others will share too, and the dominos will fall. If we stay silent, those in crisis will run to whomever is talking.

As a friend visited me from out of town one night, we sat on my couch and swapped a few stories of silly and not-so-silly choices we made in high school. A door opened for me to share my testimony with her, and I walked through it. As I spoke, her eyes filled with tears. And she told me that she too had an abortion. Other than her husband, whom she had the abortion with, I was the only person she had ever told. Shame—or shall we say Satan—kept her silent until that moment. But letting down my guard gave her the bravery to let hers down too. She cried as she spoke but felt relief knowing she wasn't alone. I was able to direct her to some postabortion counseling and pray with her. But if she hadn't heard my story, she might still feel alone and trapped. Although she ran to the lies of the abortion clinic once, I was determined to offer her transparency and truth when it was my turn. She had to know God loved her despite her choices. The proclamation of our stories and the sharing of our junk brings people out of hiding, loosening the grip Satan has on them. And God is made famous.

Countless women like her roam the world. And the church must not stay quiet while those in crisis run elsewhere for help.

I don't speak of the church as the building we meet in on Sundays but as the people that make it up. Talking about our struggles and sins is not the responsibility of the pastor and staff alone. The responsibility to extend grace and offer the forgiving love of Jesus lies with all of us. We can share our stories with anyone willing to listen—our small group, moms on a play date, and younger women coming after us. We don't force the conversation but are open to the moving of the Holy Spirit. And when prompted by Him, we are obedient to open our mouths and glorify His name.

We as His church have been cast as one body, to stand on stage and give an encore of His miraculous love. But people won't stay until the end, and may not even buy a ticket, if they can't trust we will love them regardless.

Is this hard? You bet. Will we be perfect at extending grace? No way. But I sure as heck want to do my best to try and resist the temptation to gossip and give my opinions, even if only to myself. I want to live with the perspective of what my eternal life could be like if it weren't for the Cross. And as I live with this grateful reality, I listen as Jesus does—to the sins of sinners and the confessions of Christ followers.

Imagine the church standing before an audience of broken people who have run to the body of Christ for the Answer. If this is our desire, then we, like Hosea, must be the mirror of God's grace to others. We must recognize we all deserve eternal separation from God. But only by the Cross, no merit of our own, do we get into heaven. This puts our heart on the right course to open our arms to fellow sinners. And as we talk openly about sin, even sharing our sin stories with them and God's love despite it, we become a mirror that reflects the immutable majesty and grace of Jesus Himself. And we make God famous.

Curtain.

Questions to Consider:

» Have you ever run away from the body of Christ to a "safe" place to talk about your sin?

» Who/where did you run? What made you run there and not elsewhere?

» What were you afraid of?

» Do you find that you are quick to think negatively of others when you see their sin? What sins do you think most negatively of?

» What will you do to stop this mindset?

» What do you think of the idea of being a mirror to the world of the grace of Jesus?

» Do you agree that the church as a whole should talk about sin for what it is and be a safe place where those in crisis can run?

» What does the church, as the body, need to do to achieve this?

» How will you contribute to make that happen?

SECTION 2:

YOUR GIFTS FOR THE GLORY OF GOD

God gave you and me unique, natural gifts at birth and spiritual gifts when we became believers. These gifts are not for our own benefit and applause. Rather, they are given so that when people want to give us an "Oscar" for all we've accomplished, our acceptance speech points to the Giver of the gifts. Will we be selfless enough to point the spotlight of our fame to the true Famous One?

7

She Is Fierce

Though she be but little, she is fierce.

—William Shakespeare, *A Midsummer Night's Dream*

Hermia in William Shakespeare's *A Midsummer Night's Dream* is one of my favorite roles I've ever played. Hermia is described as small, with dark hair, and fierce.

Demetrius loves Hermia, but Hermia loves Lysander. So Hermia and Lysander leave in the night to marry. But in the middle of the night, a fairy sprinkles Lysander with a love potion, causing him to fall in love with Helena, Hermia's friend. When Hermia discovers Lysander is in love with Helena, her nails come out. Hermia yells at Helena for stealing her man. Helena calls Hermia a puppet—alluding to the fact that she thinks Hermia is playing a trick on her, as both Lysander and Demetrius, who was also sprinkled with love potion, suddenly have directed their affections toward Helena. But Hermia thinks "puppet" is in reference to her height, which makes Hermia all the angrier. Hermia says she may be short, but she's tall enough to claw Helena's eyes out. Lysander and Demetrius keep Hermia from attacking Helena. Helena sees that Hermia's height is something Hermia is sensitive about, so Helena continues to push this button. About this and Hermia's temper Helena says,

```
O, when she's angry, she is keen and shrewd!
She was a vixen when she went to school;
And though she be but little, she is fierce.
```

Then Hermia lunges for Helena. And Helena, with legs longer than Hermia's, as she enjoys pointing out, runs away.

If I had to choose to live like Hermia or Helena in real life, I'd choose Hermia. I'm drawn to her passion, her desire to go after what she loves, no matter how ridiculous she looks to others, and her fighting spirit—ready to charge at anything that gets in her way. I'd like to add a touch of "think before you act" to her personality, but I love her fierceness nonetheless.

I think we need more Hermias and fewer Helenas in the world. The world doesn't need women who shrink and run away but women who stand up and walk toward the action, who believe their God is bigger than any obstacle and will come onto the stage and obediently perform the role God's given them to play.

* Two Productions, One Actor, and a Decision *

I once auditioned for a large, well-known regional theater and attended their callback. The character they were considering me for was a small role with only a few lines. This role wouldn't be too much of a stretch for me to play, but in situations like these, I try to look for opportunities to learn from the director, actors, and all involved in the production. I waited to see what their decision would be.

In the meantime, I auditioned for a second show, whose production would run at the same time as the first one. They invited me to their callbacks as well. But when I arrived for this second round of auditions, the sides (short, selected scenes from the script) of the character they had me read for said and did some things on stage that I do not say and do in real life. I had assumed the director would call me in for a different character—the character in the show who was a little more tame—but the director seemed to think I was best suited for the more provocative chick. Though a smaller theater than the one I auditioned for earlier in the week, this was a huge role. And this character was so incredibly different from me, I knew if I was cast she would stretch me as an actor beyond what I thought I could do.

I could tell at the callbacks the director was interested in me for the role. I expressed my concern over the lines and scenes, and the director was frustrated at my naivety. Wanting to impress the director, and feeling embarrassed that I was so conservative, I didn't push the subject.

I left those callbacks and asked God, if I was to be cast in one of the shows, to cast me in the show with the role He wanted me to play.

I was cast in both. And I had a big decision to make.

It is seldom that an actor is in the position of choosing which show to be a part of. More often the director is the one choosing. I felt very grateful. I consulted with other actors and directors and asked them which role they would choose if they were in my situation. Hands down they suggested I choose the larger and more challenging role and turn down the smaller role at the larger theater because of the growth they believed the role would bring me.

But when I asked God the same question, I didn't come to the same conclusion that my fellow thespians did. I sensed God was asking me to go with the smaller role at the larger theater. I knew if the audience saw me portray the more seductive role, they would see the character, but they would also see me. The patrons might assume I was OK with all of the behaviors and words I was communicating, especially because there was nothing redemptive about the role and no lesson she, or anyone else, would learn from her choices.

Though it was a long shot, I thought maybe if I called the director we could discuss editing a few of the scenes this character was in to make her more comfortable for me. I was nervous to make the call because this director had a strong, domineering personality. But I did anyway and bravely broached the topic. He let out a big, annoyed sigh, said he would think about it and get back to me.

While I waited, I had to decide which show I would choose if he told me the role needed to stay as is. I sensed God asking me to sacrifice what I wanted to do for what He wanted me to do. But I wanted to do what I wanted to do. I spent hours trying to justify why I needed to take the more challenging role. I was scared to turn it down, afraid the director would be mad. But my resistance was always met with God asking me to be brave and trust Him, so I would keep Him famous to those who observed my life, both on and off stage.

The next day, the director called and said, "No, Lisa. I need to keep the integrity of the show intact and not edit it for you. This is how the playwright would want this show produced, and it's how the audience would want to watch it as well." And although I was disappointed, he was exactly right.

So I thanked the director, explained how grateful I was for the opportunity to audition for him and potentially be in his show, but I had to decline. And he was angry with me. Very angry. As we hung up the phone, I knew he'd never cast me again.

And I accepted the walk-on role at the other theater.

Maybe, like me, God is asking you to do something for His glory that you don't want to do. Maybe He's asking you to obey Him when you want to justify why you shouldn't because it's almost always easier not to obey. You know what He's asking you to do will require guts and courage, and that scares you to death.

What is God asking you to do right now that will require you to be brave? Bravery is not just for the guys, ladies. It's for God's women too. So are you waiting in the wings, or are you passionately playing the character God's prepared for you to play?

God will ask women to stand up and be brave for His glory. He even writes about it in Scripture.

* The Fab Five *

In the first one and a half chapters of Exodus, only the second book of the Bible, God sets the stage for one of the most significant acts in the history of the Hebrew people. And He uses women for the job. And not just one woman. Five.

God's great act was for millions of bound and oppressed Hebrew slaves to walk out of Egypt into freedom. That's right. Go from chains to liberty overnight and plunder the Egyptians in the process. And God used *women* to set the stage for this amazing Exodus to take place.

God didn't give these women easy, girly tasks. Each of the assignments required bravery. They had to walk onstage and risk their lives to complete what God asked them to do. Their courage made Him famous.

The ginormous Hebrew population of 2 million (Exodus 12:37; 38:26; Numbers 1:45–47) threatened Pharaoh. A few hundred years prior, there were only 70 Hebrews in the land (Genesis 46:26). These folks took God up on His command, "Be fruitful and multiply" (Genesis 1:28). Pharaoh convinced himself if war broke out, the Hebrews would join Egypt's enemies and fight against them. So instead of persuading the Hebrew people to be forever allies with Egypt, Pharaoh made them slaves to control them. Brilliant plan. Remind me to never buy Pharaoh's book on how to run a country.

The harsh burdens would surely cut down on the slaves' quality of life and result in a lack of intimacy between spouses due to complete exhaustion. Yet God had a different plan. "But the more they were oppressed, the more they multiplied" (Exodus 1:12). Unity happened under oppression—something I should take note of as a wife.

When Pharaoh's plan didn't work, he chose another annihilation method—infanticide.

But God protected His people and used women to keep His plan from being thwarted.

SHIPHRAH AND PUAH—HEBREW MIDWIVES

Pharaoh commanded the two head Hebrew midwives to kill all baby boys as soon as they were born.

> Then the king of Egypt said to the Hebrew midwives, one of whom was named Shiphrah and the other Puah, "When you serve as midwife to the Hebrew women and see them on the birthstool, if it is a son, you shall kill him, but if it is a daughter, she shall live."
>
> —EXODUS 1:15–16

They were to kill them in secret so that the parents and relatives believed the baby had died from natural causes.

The two head midwives were probably in charge of a company of birthing assistants but refused to pass along Pharaoh's instructions.

Moses, the writer of Exodus, tells us why. "But the midwives *feared God* and did not do as the king of Egypt commanded them, but let the male children live" (Exodus 1:17, author's emphasis).

If Pharaoh found out these two women went against him, he would have killed them. Out of respect for God and a commitment to His fame, they risked everything. These women left the comfort of their seats in the wings and took their places on the stage of God's big story.

When Pharaoh noticed the midwives didn't follow his order, he asked why. "The midwives said to Pharaoh, 'Because the Hebrew women are not like the Egyptian women, for they are vigorous and give birth before the midwife comes to them'" (Exodus 1:19).

The Hebrew boy babies, including baby Moses who God would call to lead His people out of Egypt one day, were spared. God used women to make it happen. As a result, God blessed Shiphrah and Puah with families of their own (Exodus 1:21).

Killing off the legacy of the Hebrews became Pharaoh's top priority. And if slavery and the Hebrew midwives couldn't get the job done, he would have his army take over the infanticide. And so he ordered them to throw all the Hebrew baby boys into the Nile River (Exodus 1:22).

Can you imagine the heart of God as He watched babies He'd created and known before they were in their mother's womb (Jeremiah 1:5) be tossed into the river like trash?

His people needed release.

God introduced another fierce woman to carry out His plan.

JOCHEBED—MOSES'S MOTHER

Perhaps countless parents died protecting their boys as the Egyptian military came to steal babies from Hebrew homes. Moses's mother, Jochebed* (Exodus 6:20), risked her life for her own baby boy.

Pronounced: yō·keh'·ved

She and her husband kept him hidden for three months (Exodus 2:2). Hebrews 11:23 tells us Moses's parents found the courage to hide him because they trusted God and were not afraid of the king's law.

When they could no longer hide him, Jochebed had an idea that forced her to walk onstage and perform one of the bravest acts God has ever asked of a mother.

She made a waterproof basket, placed Moses inside, and set the basket among the reeds of the crocodile-infested Nile riverbank (Exodus 2:3). Pharaoh would kill him otherwise. At least this way he had a chance and maybe a few more moments away from the murderers. As she turned to leave him there, too sick with grief to stay, she convinced herself she'd never see him again. She parted ways with her child, with slim hope.

She pleaded with God to send someone to save him from his watery grave. And since God's plan can't be thwarted, someone did.

HATSHEPSUT—PHARAOH'S DAUGHTER

God introduced another woman to save Moses's life. At this point, she was the only person with enough clout to rescue the boy—Pharaoh's daughter, Hatshepsut*.

people knew her as a very forceful woman who even assumed co-regency with Thutmose III, ruling as the fifth Pharaoh from 1503–1482 BC.

While coming down to the riverbank to bathe, Hatshepsut saw the basket and sent her servant girl to bring the basket to her. When she opened the basket, baby Moses lay there crying, and though he was Hebrew, she felt sorry for him and wanted to take him as her own son (Exodus 2:5–6, 10). This confident woman probably didn't care what her father thought about bringing a Hebrew baby to live in their house.

Although she followed gods and worshipped idols, and she didn't risk doing anything brave for God, God used her anyway. God will use women who love Him and women who don't love Him to accomplish His purposes. I just never want Him to skip over me because I'm not brave enough to come out onto the stage.

MIRIAM—MOSES'S SISTER

Moses's sister Miriam stayed by the river to watch what might happen to him. As Miriam watched Pharaoh's daughter in the Nile, she knew this was her opportunity. This was her chance to make God famous, though she would risk her life to do so. With great heroism, Miriam approached Pharaoh's daughter and asked if she could find a nurse for the baby. And Hatshepsut said, "Go" (Exodus 2:8).

Jochebed's daughter and Pharaoh's daughter were just as opposite in rank in the eyes of Egypt and Israel as me and the president. As a slave, Miriam bolstered significant courage to speak to Hatshepsut. Her bold move brought a situation Jochebed could not have imagined when she hid Moses.

Miriam brought Jochebed to Hatshepsut. Unbeknownst to Hatshepsut, she commanded the mother of this baby to nurse him and even offered to pay her money to do so (Exodus 2:9). *Say what?*

Dr. Thomas Constable, founder of Dallas Theological Seminary's Center for Biblical Studies, says:

> Several women were involved in the events surrounding Moses's birth: the midwives, Pharaoh's daughter, Moses's sister, and Jochebed. How ironic it was that women, whom Egyptian and Israelite men looked down on as less significant than themselves, should have been responsible for saving Israel's savior! Truly the hand of God is evident.

God could have used men, as He does elsewhere in Scripture, to preserve the nation of Israel. But He chose to use women five times in a few short verses. Whenever we see repetition in Scripture, God is making a point. Whether He repeats words or themes, God knows repetition provides emphasis. God's point was that women are important, capable, and strong to further His plan—and make Him famous. Though small in stature among the human species, He created women to be fierce for His fame.

* What If? *

But imagine if these women stood backstage, too scared to walk past the curtain? If Shiphrah and Puah had stayed in the wings, thousands of babies would have died. Moses might have been one of them.

If Jochebed watched God's production from offstage, Moses would have died as the army searched their home because she was too scared to hide him. If he survived a house search, standing in the wings would have meant she would have been too scared to risk her family's life to build a basket for him, and it would have only been a matter of time before the army found him.

If Miriam allowed worry to make her pace backstage, she would have run home in fear and never have spoken up to Hatshepsut. Moses wouldn't have had a chance to grow into what God would call him to do.

Waiting in the wings will limit the ways we actively and obediently participate in His work. But walking past that curtain line and onto the stage makes God famous and allows others to make Him famous too.

* Our Actions Make Others Brave *

Have you ever considered how our actions allow others the opportunity to play their role in God's big story? All of these women had a chance to walk into God's plan because the woman before them acted out her faith. Had one stopped in fear, the next one wouldn't have had her chance. We have an obligation to step forward to participate with God and for God, to pave the way for others to do the same. Who knows who could be used by Him because of our tremendous faith?

And who knows who might find his or her own bravery as he or she watches us walk onstage? Just like Miriam, who watched her mom's selfless bravery, garnered tremendous courage when it was her turn.

What is God asking you to do right now that will require you to be brave?

* God Often Blesses Our Obedience *

Rehearsals were about to begin for the show at the larger theater when I received a call from the theater company. They had a certain budget they were forced to spend on actors' salaries in order to stay in compliance with the actors' union. They hadn't spent the max yet, and asked if they could increase my salary by double to get them to the minimum standard. I took them up on it. And on the same call, they told me they were giving me a different role, a much larger one, if I was OK with that. And I took them up on that one too.

I was obedient to be brave and risked embarrassment, risked never working at the smaller theater, and risked rumors being spread about me, so that I could do what I knew God wanted me to do. And He blessed my bravery just like He blessed Shiprah and Puah with families of their own when they displayed their bravery for His glory.

God may not bless us like this every time we are obedient, but I believe He delights in showing Himself off to us when we bravely show Him off to the world.

* No More Stage Fright *

Are you waiting in the wings, too scared to come onstage? Do you know God is asking you to do something brave, but the wings feel safer? Less risk, more comfort. Do you watch others shine for God onstage but you find good company with other scared souls backstage? Maybe you've convinced yourself the wings are an OK place to be.

But imagine if, when your name was called, you bravely walked past the curtain. Imagine if you pushed back the stage fright and took the role. Imagine how God could use you to stand centerstage and make Him famous. Imagine how your bravery might enlist other women to do the same.

I don't want to be another woman waiting in the wings.

It's time to quit standing by, ladies. It's time to see where we do our best work for God and where God wants us to be is not watching from backstage. It's not just giving standing ovations to others who mesmerize us with their talents. It's centerstage, embracing the role He's given us, and then pointing the spotlight where it belongs. On Him.

God may have made you little among "men," but He made you fierce. We must be brave and courageous, recognizing we were created as women by God Himself for such a time as this. God wants to use women to make His name famous.

Do you need to start that nonprofit you've dreamed of running for years? Do you need to write the book God won't leave you alone about? Do you need to say yes to the lesser role to show God and others you're willing to be obedient no matter what?

You may need to enlist some people who believe in you more than you believe in yourself to encourage you to get the job done. Tell them what God's calling you to do, and ask them to hold you accountable until you walk onstage and get the job done.

God might not ask you to risk your physical life to fulfill His plan like He did with the women in Exodus. At the same time, He just might. But regardless, He asks you to risk your daily spiritual life as you fight the enemy whose greatest fear is that you would rise up from the wings and make God famous.

Satan lies to you about who you are and how God could use you. Satan stands next to you, leans into your ear, and uses others to shout in agreement that because you're a woman, God can't and won't use you to accomplish His purposes.

Don't let another day go by that you agree with him. It's time to walk onto that stage. It's time to be fierce for His fame.

Questions to Consider:

» Have you ever felt like you're waiting in the wings? Why?

» What is God asking you to do right now that will require you to be brave?

» How do you feel about that?

» Even after acknowledging your feelings, what might still keep you backstage?

» How will you fight back to ensure you do what God's asking you to do?

» Who do you need to enlist to help you?

8

Find Your Light

"Find your light!": What a director will say to an actor during rehearsal. This phrase lets the actor know they need to move a few steps in any direction until they feel the light from above shining on them, illuminating their faces so the audience can see them.

The place God calls you to is the place where your deep gladness and the world's deep hunger meet.
—Frederick Buechner

There's a lot to think about as an actor—your lines, timing an entrance, remembering to turn your mic off before going to the bathroom, and hitting your mark on the stage so you can find your light. An actor finds their light in rehearsal so that by the time the performance comes, they know exactly where to stand in order for the light to hit them perfectly. If a director says, "Find your light," it's because the audience can't see the actor because he or she is in the shadows. So the performer moves around a few steps until they feel the warmth of the light on their face. Now the audience can see their full performance on stage.

So it is with the gifts given to us by God. Like the light from above on a stage, the gifts are there, we just need to find them. And when we do, the audience sees the glory of God through our lives.

* Finding My Light *

I was a dancer from the age of three until I was 23. I loved to dance, but I was by no means Baryshnikov. Like, not even close. I struggled to pick up choreography quickly, and though I worked to become limber, my ligaments wouldn't follow my will, and my stiffness hindered my performance. But I did shine as a dancer—in my upper body. It was thrilling for me to communicate, eyeball to eyeball with audience members, the lyrics of the song's joyous or tragic meaning through my arms, torso, and especially my face.

After a recital when I was a young teenager, a mom of a fellow dancer came up to me and, God bless her, tried to compliment my performance. She said, "Now not everyone can do the choreography with ease, but I still can't take my eyes off you. You describe the song to us through your facial expressions, and I'm mesmerized." I still remember feeling like someone understood my love of the theatrics and the stage and the stories longing to be told—even if my muscles didn't stretch to fit.

Dance was not going to be something I would make a career out of, that's for sure. And like a good, observant parent, my mom saw this too. To set me up for success, one day she said to my 11-year-old self, "Lisa, let's try a backup."

So I auditioned—no wait—*tried out* for a select volleyball team. I was so bad, y'all, that I didn't even make the team with the girls my age. I had to play with the girls a full grade younger than me. And even then, I warmed the bench. I hated volleyball, but my mom insisted I try one more year. So when middle school tryouts came, I was there. At my school there were the A, B, C, and D teams. Those who loved volleyball and had been playing on select teams with girls their own age made the A team. The D team, however, consisted of players who were artistically inclined but whose parents had said, "Let's try for a backup."

My inability to get any serve over the net, my horrible bumping skills, and my constant complaining drove my mom to release me back to the stage.

When I went to high school a few years later, I auditioned for my first play and thought heaven had come to earth. This was my happy place.

I kept dancing, but I loved the theater. I got my degree in theater, and after I graduated, people actually paid me to perform.

But then God showed me how He wanted to use these gifts for His glory in a new way.

Early in our marriage, Markus and I lived in Los Angeles and attended a church there. As a couple without kids at the time, we were a part of the young marrieds' ministry. One Sunday, the small group of six couples was extended the opportunity to share personal stories of God's redemption. We were told to raise our hands if we wanted to share. As I contemplated sharing, my stomach flip-flopped between nervousness and excitement. I raised my hand and told God's radical story of amazing grace in my life.

I spoke, and people listened to the transformational power of God. Words fell out of my mouth uninhibited, and thoughts came to me that I never had before. He took control and made Himself famous as people were encouraged and heard His story of how there's no sin too great that will halt the love of God for them.

I realized I had found my light and couldn't wait to stand "on stage" and make Him famous again.

It became a spotlight I'm addicted to. God used the natural gifts He had given me—that of communicating and being comfortable in front of people—to inform the spiritual gift of exhortation (to encourage, strengthen, instruct, and teach as seen in 2 Timothy 4:2 and Titus 2:11–15) that He had also given me when I became a believer.

* Finding Your Light *

Did you know that all of us have been given a gift to be used by God for His glory? Yep, you too. The Bible is clear.

{ *As each has received a gift, use it to serve one another, as good stewards of God's varied grace: whoever speaks, as one who speaks oracles of God; whoever serves, as one who serves by the strength that God supplies—in order that in everything God may be glorified through Jesus Christ. To him belong glory and dominion forever and ever. Amen.* }

—1 PETER 4:10–11 *(author's emphasis)*

We are given our spiritual gifts so we can help each other, meaning fellow believers (v. 10), so they can be encouraged in their faith in God (Romans 1:11–12) but also so that God receives the glory due Him as we use the spiritual gifts only He can give (1 Peter 4:11). Pastor and author John Piper says, "God's aim in giving us gifts, and in giving us the faith to exercise them, is that His glory might be displayed. He wants us and the world to marvel at Him and to think He is fantastic."

But not all of us are using our gifts. Why? We might compare ourselves with others and become discouraged when our gifts aren't as showy as someone else's.

Like a lady recently said to me after I spoke at an event on this subject, "I used to think my backstage gift was boring and second string." This may be how the world sees gifts, as we often applaud the onstage gifts before we applaud the backstage ones. But this is not how God sees our gifts. He doesn't rank them like we do. God wants to use our gifts to encourage others and bring Himself glory, even if we don't get the cheers everyone else does.

Others of us may not be using our gifts because we don't know what our gifts are. While the inclination of our heart would be to encourage each other and glorify God through our activities, if they aren't our spiritual gifts, we may be wasting our time playing volleyball instead of performing theater.

So how do we discover what God has gifted us to do? Do we take another spiritual gifts test, personality quiz, or strengths inventory? Maybe. But if that's not working for us, what if instead of taking another test, maybe we just ask ourselves a few questions and pay a little attention to our lives? In the following paragraphs, I've come up with a few questions you can ask yourself as you seek to discover how God has spiritually gifted you or as you ask Him to confirm His gifting in your life.

》 What activity, when completed, leaves you with a "high," and you can't wait to do again?

I don't mean like sitting by yourself at Starbucks with a *Southern Living* magazine in hand, enjoying a pumpkin spice latte in the fall—although I'm sure I could convince someone this was my gift. But what activities, when completed, make you feel on top of the world? Serving in the missions ministry at church? Discipling a younger Christian? Watching a friend's kids? Hosting an event? Volunteering at a homeless shelter?

When I walk off a platform after I speak, I'm on a spiritual high. I come home, collapse on the couch, and proceed to tell Markus about the event. Though physically exhausted, I'm spiritually energized. I think, *I can't wait to do this again.* This is the continued, active presence of the Holy Spirit within me, giving me deep fulfillment as I used His gifts so I will have the courage to do it next time. All for His glory.

》 What comes naturally to you but not to everyone?

When you're using your gift, others may look at you with their jaw gaped open and say, "How do you do what you do? There's no way I could ever do that." While you think, *This is nothing. It comes so naturally to me.* It's important to bookmark these times because maybe these are signposts from God that you're on the right track to figuring out how He wants to use you to make His name great.

Of course, you will need to work on honing your gift and growing in it. And of course, you may be crazy nervous, anxious, and excited using your gifts, but that doesn't mean you're on the wrong track. Just because we have butterflies in our stomachs doesn't mean we aren't gifted. Anxiety may be a sign that you need to give this over to God and quit worrying so much about what people think.

》 What do you spend your time on?

My mom always said, "We put our time where our priorities are." When trying to figure out your gift, make note of how you spend your time. We perform many tasks because we need to fulfill responsibilities. But your gift is not another thing to add to your to-do list. Our God-given gifts are activities we want to spend time on and make time for.

I've noticed I spend a lot of time preparing for a talk. I don't approach the preparation begrudgingly or wish I were doing something else. Quite the opposite. In addition to the actual speaking event, I enjoy the time I spend preparing.

Do you host events at your house and spend hours making food and decorating? Or maybe you find that you meet regularly with someone struggling in their walk with God. You also notice that you do deep biblical research and spend lots of time in prayer before you meet with them.

We spend time on what's important to us. God wired us this way so that we will continue to learn and perfect the gifts He's given us.

» What do people cheer you on about?

When we operate in the center of our God-given gifts, people notice. They might come up and compliment us on a gift we used or tell us how we impacted them.

Maybe they notice your incredible discernment, your knack for administration, or your stand-alone leadership. People will say, "This is your gift," "You are very talented in this area," "You need to keep doing this," "Thank you for what you did. It had a tremendous effect on me." What are some areas of your life where people have repeatedly encouraged you? Where's the consistency? If you can't think of times in the past, pay attention in the future as different people cheer you on.

» What are you asked to do again and again?

Do you find you are asked to do the same things over and over—lead a group, give your advice, or speak at events? Pay attention to this because it probably means you're gifted in that area. Your gift is needed and valuable. People take note of what they believe we're gifted in and ask us to use the gift, even if we're clueless.

» What do you sit around and dream about?

What do you sit around and wish you could do? *If only the right doors would open. If only I had a different job. If only I had more money. If only things were different, I would do (fill in the blank).* What do you dream of doing? What do you dream about happening in the world, community, or church? Your dreams may be the key to your gifts.

But here's a caution—if we get caught up in what we wish we *were* doing, then we can become bitter about where we are *now*. Instead, ask God to give you opportunities to use your gifts in whatever situation you currently find yourself, even if it may look a little different from the image in your mind. And then patiently and obediently wait for Him to release you into the dream He's put within you.

» What would you do for free?

If you had all the money you needed to keep things keepin' on in your life, what would you do for free? Because instead of the money, the joy the Holy Spirit gives you is the payout. I would speak to groups every day for free if I could afford to. Is there something you would do for free? If so, then you're probably pretty passionate about it. So passionate, in fact, that it just might be your gift.

* Craving the Light *

Can you imagine God releasing His power through you? Can you imagine discovering your gifts and using them for the good of others and the glory of God?

May we not assume God has buried our gifts in a deeply hidden treasure chest, forcing us to go on a massive treasure hunt to discover them. Instead, may we realize our gifts through the simple acts of asking questions and paying attention, knowing God wants us to discover and use our gifts. And as we find and use those Spirit-empowered gifts, may we crave this spotlight so that we can stand under the warmth of the Light, radiating the fame of God to all who will listen.

Questions to Consider:

» Do you know how God has gifted you?

» If not, did you get an idea of how you might be gifted as you read the questions? What came to mind?

» If you do know your gifts, were those gifts affirmed as you reviewed the questions in this chapter? How?

» Sometimes we don't think highly of ourselves, which keeps us from believing and seeing that we could be gifted by God. We need a gentle push. Who knows you best? If you trust them, ask them to help you highlight areas in your life in which you shine. Then pay attention to those shining moments as they present themselves in the future. And you just might find your gift.

9

The Go-See

Go-see: a modeling audition for print work for a billboard, magazine, etc.

Before I shaped you in the womb, I knew all about you. Before you saw the light of day, I had holy plans for you: A prophet to the nations—that's what I had in mind for you.

—JEREMIAH 1:5 *THE MESSAGE*

A go-see is to modeling what an audition is to acting. The model *goes* to a photographer's studio or casting facility, and they're *seen* and photographed for the client. Then, the client decides if the model is the best choice to promote their product, hence the name, go-see. There is possibly nothing in the business that compares people more solely on the basis of their looks than the go-see. The model is typically not asked to read from a script, improv a scene, or show any talent whatsoever. They are simply to stand and look beautiful. After the models have come and gone, the photography director and the client compare the models' pictures taken at the go-see. Depending on their face, body type, height, weight, hair, and overall vibe, they choose or reject the model.

No wonder there are so many models with low self-esteem in this business.

Unless the client is looking for "moms," I'm hardly ever chosen when I attend a go-see. Most of the time, they are looking for tall, lean women. I'm 5'3" and curvy. Enough said.

Just like a go-see, we compare ourselves to people all day long. I know I do—a superfit woman at the gym, a seemingly amazing wife in a fiction book, or a confident, real-life mom in the booth next to me at Chick-fil-A.

* My Today Show Friend *

Just the other day, I stalked a model friend of mine on Facebook. (You stalk people on Facebook too—you know you do.) This gal flits back and forth between modeling shoots in New York City and Dallas. She posted pictures of herself backstage in the hair and makeup chair on the *Today* show, yet again, as she prepped to model jeans for a segment with Kathie Lee and Hoda. She has a flat in NYC and an apartment in Dallas. I imagined what it might be like to be her and became a little jealous of her easy, exciting life. Oh, to have a talent agent in Dallas and one in NYC, paid-for flights between both, *per diem*, walks through Central Park with your dog and a coffee after the morning segment, and out for an evening with friends at a hot new restaurant in either city. What a life!

After a day or so of wishing I was her, reality hit me as hard as a rent bill in Greenwich Village. If I were her, I wouldn't have my husband or my kids and my messy, nonadventurous-but-beautiful life. And even more sobering, I'll never be her because my body frame is the pendulum-swing opposite of her long-legged one. So even if I worked hard to have her career, I wouldn't because I can't do anything about being vertically challenged.

But then I compare myself to people who are doing what I could do . . . if only the right doors would open. I compare myself to women who speak to a national audience, with hundreds of thousands of social media followers, more hits on their websites, and an even bigger blogging platform. I look at their numerous speaking engagements, their offers to go overseas—fully paid—to research their next book. As their publications line the bookstore shelves, I pale in comparison.

How do I respond? Instead of listening to these gals as they communicate on social media or on a stage, I'm discouraged by my lack of knowledge.

Instead of watching their journey and learning from them, I'm pre-occupied by my "green-ness."

Instead of cheering them on, I'm sidetracked by my jealousy.

Now convicted, I'm reminded that the Bible is full of people playing the comparison game. And nothing goes well for the jealous.

》 Cain wished he had the blessing of God.

》 Jacob wished he had Esau's birthright.

》 Sarah wished she could have children like Hagar.

》 The Israelites wished they had the wealth of the Canaanites.

》 David wished he had Uriah's wife.

》 Each of Jesus' disciples wished he were a different disciple.

》 Judas wished he had more money.

》 And Lisa wishes she were someone else.

When I'm distracted by who I am not, I lose focus of who I am. God doesn't want me to be another woman doing what He's called her to do. If I'm *her*, then I'm not *me*. And God created me to be me, not someone else. My comparison game is like telling the Creator He has my life all wrong, and I know better than He does.

* Not Satisfied *

Maybe you compare yourself to others and think, *If only I were someone else. If only I were in a different situation. If only I had a different life. Then God could do wonders through me. Then I'd be happy.* When we are preoccupied by our insecurities and debilitated by our distractions, we can't be about the business of doing what He's called us to do to make Him famous with our lives. And Satan will be right there trying to divert our hearts with deceptions.

I believe the reason we compare ourselves to others is because we're not satisfied with who we are. We're not satisfied with what we look like, how we're gifted, or the life we're living. We are not satisfied with what God's given us. And we are simply not grateful. So we compare our lives with others and imagine ourselves in a different situation. Because somehow we're convinced we've come up short. And I don't mean 5'3", like me.

As a result, we live depressed and often useless in the fight to make God famous.

Mankind's lust after what we don't have has been a thorn in our side from the beginning of time.

* Adam and Eve and Everything *

In the first pages of Bible, we observe God beautifully conceiving the world, including the dry land and its animals, fruit trees, and plants. He separates the waters into seas and fills them with creatures swimming within and birds flying above. We watch as He divides the day from night with the sun and moon and places twinkling stars in the sky. There was no death on this majestic earth, only life. And I'm sure to take a look at this perfection of a planet, one would think, *What more could be added?* But God had one more glorious addition.

God created man, made in His image (Genesis 1:26), distinctly different from the rest of the world He made. God would have a relationship of close fellowship with mankind. So He created the first man, Adam, and placed him in the Garden of Eden, where he was to work the garden. God brought every animal and bird He had made to Adam for him to name. What ownership Adam must have felt over this amazing creation.

There were two trees in the middle of Eden, the tree of life and the tree of the knowledge of good and evil. Adam was to enjoy all of Eden, with one exception—he was not to eat from the tree of the knowledge of good and evil, or he would die.

God looked at Adam, and He saw that Adam was alone and needed a partner. So He caused a deep sleep to come upon Adam—

let's call this the earliest form of anesthesia—and took a rib from Adam and made Eve, his female partner. The Bible says He brought her to Adam, like a gift. And Genesis 2:25—which is my husband's favorite verse by the way—says, "And the man and his wife were both naked and were not ashamed."

God commanded them to have lots of babies and fill the earth with little Adam Juniors and Princess Eves. He directed them to make all of the earth's resources beneficial to themselves. God gave them *everything*. As I studied Genesis 1, I noticed how much God gave Adam and Eve, noted by each time He uses the word, "every."

> And God blessed them. And God said to them, "Be fruitful and multiply and fill the earth and subdue it, and have dominion over the fish of the sea and over the birds of the heavens and over *every* living thing that moves on the earth." And God said, "Behold, I have given you *every* plant yielding seed that is on the face of all the earth, and *every* tree with seed in its fruit. You shall have them for food."

— GENESIS 1:28–29 *(author's emphasis)*

God generously gave Adam and Eve *everything* they needed and more.

He continues expressing His mighty generosity to the rest of His creation.

> "And to *every* beast of the earth and to *every* bird of the heavens and to *everything* that creeps on the earth, *everything* that has the breath of life, I have given *every* green plant for food." And it was so. And God saw *everything* that he had made, and behold, it was *very* good.

— GENESIS 1:30–31 *(author's emphasis)*

God saw His world, His people, and His provisions for both, and it couldn't get better. Maybe we can assume Adam and Eve thought the same. That is, until they were shown what they didn't have, and all of the sudden, what they *did* have wasn't all that good anymore.

* Satan Enters Stage Left *

Satan comes to Eve and immediately tries to dismantle her resolve that God is good by suggesting that He is unfair.

I can just hear their conversation. From what Genesis 3:1–5 tells us, I imagine it went something like, "Now really, Eve. Did God actually say that you and Adam are not to eat the fruit off of *any* tree in the garden?"

"No, we can eat the fruit of any tree. But there is one fruit tree in the middle of the garden that we can't eat from. Oh, and we can't touch it either. Or we will die."

But God didn't say not to touch it, did He? He only said not to *eat* from it (2:17). Has she already decided that God's instructions are up for human interpretation? Appears so.

Satan continues to suggest that she is missing out. I can hear his lying, manipulative tongue saying, "Oh no, Eve, you won't die! God is just selfish because He knows that when you eat the fruit of that tree, your eyes will be opened. Up until now, God has closed your eyes. But when you eat the fruit of that tree, you will *be like God*, knowing good and evil."

A desire to *be like God*, and therefore have more than what she had, is the only weapon Satan needed. Satan knew that a desire to be like God would be extremely tempting. After all, this same desire led to his own downfall and got him kicked out of heaven (Isaiah 14:12–15). Eve is now convinced there's more that she's not been given. And she goes from trusting God to doubting Him. Her heart is not in a place of humility, recognizing that she needs to be grateful for what she *does* have rather than focus on what she doesn't. And because she doesn't recognize the lie of the enemy, she now thinks God is keeping something from her. She wants what God's not given her, what's not hers to have, and she thinks she can't live without it.

{ *So when the woman saw that the tree was good for food, and that it was a delight to the eyes, and that the tree was to be desired to make one wise, she took of its fruit and ate, and she also gave some to her husband who was with her, and he ate.* }

— GENESIS 3:6

* Sin Enters the World and Now Death with It *

Adam and Eve had been given everything God deemed they needed. They were content . . . until they saw what they didn't have. And immediately their eyes were opened, but they weren't opened to be like God, as Satan said they would be. No, their eyes were opened to see that they were now even further from God and they were ashamed of themselves and their nakedness. And they knew they were wrong. So they sewed fig leaves together to cover their naked bodies, and they hid from God amongst the trees. The trees that God intended for man to admire and see as a reflection of His goodness were now used to keep God from seeing them (3:7–8).

God blessed Adam and Eve abundantly. But their desire for what wasn't theirs led to an abrupt stop and diversion from God's path for them.

I wonder if God, though omniscient and knowing this would happen, looked on all of this with a deeply broken heart, so achingly sad that His plan wasn't considered good enough by His creation. "Have you eaten of the tree of which I commanded you not to eat? . . . What is this you have done?" (2:11, 13).

A lack of gratitude kept Adam and Eve from living in a sin-free, death-free world where communion with God was like walking alongside Him in a garden. A desire for what wasn't theirs kept them, and now the rest of the world, from having a guaranteed, healthy, and functioning relationship between a husband and wife. It also resulted in pain in childbirth as a punishment. A heart of comparison took the work that God intended to bring joy to the man and made it unpleasant and toilsome.

They listened to the enemy, who told them that what God had given them wasn't enough.

And so they forgot the Lord and His perfect provision.

> *Give me neither poverty nor riches, but give me only my daily bread. Otherwise, I may have too much and disown you and say, "Who is the Lord?" Or I may become poor and steal, and so dishonor the name of my God.*

— PROVERBS 30:8–9 (NIV)

And like Adam and Eve, when we compare what we don't have with what we could have and go after and get what God never intended for us to take, we will have a moment of instant gratification. I'm sure the fruit was delicious. But we will wind up empty and worse off than we were before.

* God's Success *

God isn't concerned about my number of blog followers, whether I publish countless books, speak to a stadium full of women, or even book a national commercial. But God will hold me accountable for making Him famous while I live—to my kids, my husband, my neighbors, to the cashier at the grocery store, and the employee at the drive-through. While I need to be active in moving forward with what God has entrusted me with, numbers won't determine success in His eyes.

When we are ungrateful for what God's given us and we compare ourselves to what others have, we become preoccupied by what *they* are doing and how God could be glorifying Himself through *them* instead of focusing on what *we* are doing and how He can glorify Himself through *us*. And we may go after something God never intended for us to have.

If we spend countless minutes, days, months, or years distracted by all we wish we were doing and wish we had, we will completely miss out on all God has for us to do right now. If we get wrapped up in if-onlys, we will miss out on today. And we will show God how ungrateful we are for what He *has* blessed us with.

God wants you to embrace you—in whatever stage of life you're in, right in the middle of your gifting, so He can get to work using you now. He didn't give you someone else's gifts or attributes, because they weren't for you. They were for *them*. And He didn't give *them* certain gifts or attributes, because they were for *you*.

Here's the truth, sister. God made you. He has you where He has you for a reason, and He desires to use you there. And unless we embrace this, we will continue to spin our wheels in frustration and bitterness and live in if-onlys. And we will continue to live in a world full of women who live in competition with each other. We must instead be content with the gifts, lifestyle, stage of life, and bodies we have, or we will waste the time God has given us. When Christ comes back, I don't want Him to catch me looking on Facebook at my NYC and Dallas model friend, wishing I had her life.

Instead, let's refuse to be preoccupied by insecurities, lies, and comparisons. Because I am a work of art, created by the Creator of all things, Sustainer of all things, and Redeemer of all things to do what He has in mind for me to do to make Him famous. And so are you.

Let's not go after what's not ours to have but only after what God intends for us, knowing that maybe we're exactly where He wants us.

Questions to Consider:

>> Whom do you compare yourself to?

>> What do they have that you wish you had?

>> How has comparing yourself to them sidetracked you and slowed you down from living to make God famous?

>> Have comparisons caused you to go after what's not yours to have?

>> Do you believe God's given you enough?

>> If you decided to live a life where you believed God had given you enough, how would you live differently?

» How do you see that God has made you unique?

» How can you cheer people on instead of comparing yourself to them?

» How can you use what He's given you—no more, no less—for His glory?

10

Booking the Job

"You booked the job.": what an agent says to an actor whom the producers and directors hire for a TV, film, or commercial role.

t's wonderful to hear, "You booked the job," after auditioning for a commercial. It allows me to use my gifts, bring home a paycheck, and build relationships with actors and crew.

Booking a job means I've been chosen to play a specific role. It means that out of all the other talent, they chose me because not only did I look the part but also they thought I could deliver a convincing performance that would clearly communicate the idea of their advertising campaign.

This process reminds me of how God chooses us to do big things for His name and His fame. He selects us for a specific role because He knows we are capable of delivering a convincing performance that will clearly communicate what He's advertising—His glory.

Yet the analogy of booking a job and doing what God's called me to do breaks down right here because I usually feel very adequate to portray the character on a commercial. I'm confident, though still a little nervous, that I can do that job—just like you may feel in your work, whatever and wherever that work may be. But when *God* asks me to do big things for His name, I feel very inadequate. God often asks us to do jobs we are not confident doing. He does this because if I can do it in my own strength, then I'll more likely take the credit. But if I complete the task that I feel inadequate doing, I'll point people back to Him as the reason it got done in the first place. And He will get the glory. So He asks me to do things that only He can do through me.

When God called me to write the proposal for this book, I thought He was crazy.

I only saw roadblocks. I'd never written anything. I questioned God, *Who am I? I'm not a writer, I'm an actor. I act out what people write, but I'm not an author. I hated English class in school. I don't know the first thing about sentence structure or grammar. How do I write a book proposal? I'm completely inadequate for this assignment. I don't have time—I have kids. And come to think about it, You gave these little boogers to me, so my "time constraints" are Your fault. Thanks, but like the investors say on* Shark Tank, *"I'm out."*

Maybe God is asking you to do something too. But you make excuse after excuse because you feel inadequate.

Sometimes we toss in the towel before trying. *Why would God call me? I'm completely insufficient. There's no way I can do this.*

But God won't leave you alone. He's like my kids who nag me to get out of bed on Saturday morning for a donut run. He just keeps on pestering until you throw off the covers and take your nasty, morning breath, slippered, sweatpants-donning, and, hopefully, bra-wearing self out the door.

He's booked you for the job. Your heart is moved each and every time you think about it, but the journey to get it done overwhelms you. Because you feel so inadequate. So when God calls us to something, how do we get past these feelings to press forward?

Luckily for us, we can find some courage as we dive deeper into Moses's story.

When God booked Moses for the ridiculously overwhelming job of leading His people out of slavery, Moses was at an all-time emotional low—like my Dallas Cowboys at the end of every season in recent memory. Moses felt inadequate, but he hadn't always felt this way.

✳ Moses's Early Years ✳

As we learned in chapter 7, Pharaoh's daughter sent baby Moses back to live with his Hebrew parents after she discovered him in a basket in the reeds of the Nile River. But there was a catch. After Moses was weaned, he would have to come back to the house of Pharaoh to live as Pharaoh's grandson. The period of time Moses lives with his birth parents could have been as little as 2–3 years or as many as 12 years. Did Jochebed nurse him that entire time? I dunno. But if I knew I had to drop my baby off at some king's palace, knowing I'd probably never see him again, I just might tell Pharaoh's daughter he was hard to wean.

Moses's parents knew they would eventually send him back to live in idol-worshipping, godless Egypt. So they needed to drill into his head that his people believed in the God of his ancestors—Abraham, Isaac, and Jacob—the one true God. They probably told him of the Abrahamic covenant that promised slavery wasn't the end of the Hebrew people. And of the stories of Joseph from more than 400 years prior and the great favor the kind Pharaoh gave the Hebrews because of Joseph's influence and position.

> *Then Joseph settled his father and his brothers and gave them a possession in the land of Egypt, in the best of the land, in the land of Rameses, as Pharaoh had commanded. . . . Thus Israel settled in the land of Egypt, in the land of Goshen. And they gained possessions in it, and were fruitful and multiplied greatly.*
>
> —GENESIS 47:11, 27

Moses's parents probably told him that the Pharaoh of Joseph's day showed great compassion to the Hebrew people.

> *Then Pharaoh said to Joseph, "Your father and your brothers have come to you. The land of Egypt is before you. Settle your father and your brothers in the best of the land. Let them settle in the land of Goshen, and if you know any able men among them, put them in charge of my livestock."*
>
> —GENESIS 47:5–6

But the Pharaoh whose home *Moses* was to grow up in was nothing like the Pharaoh of Joseph's day, "There arose a new king over Egypt, who did not know Joseph" (Exodus 1:8). And thus began a period of 430 years of slavery for the Hebrews (Exodus 12:41 and Galatians 3:17). Maybe Moses's parents told him, "Be careful, my son, that you never identify yourself with the godless Egypt or the Pharaoh in whose home you will reside. You are a Hebrew; let no one tell you otherwise. The power of our God is with you. And the Almighty has great plans for you."

They wanted to make sure that when they dropped him off at the doorstep of Pharaoh's home, Moses would know who he was and Whom he belonged to.

Hebrews 11:24 says, "Moses, when he was grown up, refused to be called the son of Pharaoh's daughter." Moses's Egyptian mom gave him many names that referenced Egyptian gods. So when he "refused to be called the son of Pharaoh's daughter," he dropped these names because he didn't want to identify himself as an Egyptian.

He was well educated and highly esteemed. As the adopted son of Pharaoh's daughter, Moses enjoyed the highest privileges in his education. In commenting on Moses's training, Stephen said that he "was instructed in all the wisdom of the Egyptians, and he was mighty in words and deeds" (Acts 7:22). Though a Hebrew in a foreign land, he really had everything going for him. He was comfortable, had anything he wanted, was educated, and respected. But there was something that left him uneasy about his posh life in Egypt.

Moses saw his Hebrew brothers and sisters beaten and whipped and working for a king who believed he owned them like property. But in fact, they were owned by the King of kings, who had not forgotten them, who heard their painful cries, and who had plans for their deliverance.

{ *One day . . . [Moses] went out to his people and looked on their*
burdens, and he saw an Egyptian beating a Hebrew, one of his
people. *He looked this way and that, and seeing no one, he*
struck down the Egyptian and hid him in the sand. }

—EXODUS 2:11–12 *(author's emphasis)*

Once again, we see God using repetition to make a point—
"his people, his people."

Acts 7:25 says that Moses believed "his brothers would understand God was giving them salvation by his hand." But they didn't.

{ *When he went out the next day, behold, two Hebrews were*
struggling together. And he said to the man in the wrong, "Why
do you strike your companion?" He answered, "Who made you
a prince and a judge over us? Do you mean to kill me as you
killed the Egyptian?" }

—EXODUS 2:13–14

Most likely the Hebrew slaves didn't see Moses as one of their own people, as Moses saw them. Though they probably knew he was Hebrew, to them he was "Egyptian" and a traitor.

When Pharaoh found out Moses killed an Egyptian, Pharaoh sought to kill him. Exiled, Moses fled to the Hebrew land of Midian and the land of his great discouragement.

* Midian *

The 40 years Moses lived in the land of Midian were years of bitter humiliation. He gave expression to his feelings by naming his first son Gershom* (Exodus 2:22), meaning "banishment" or "a stranger there."

pronounced: gay-resh-ome

He was a shepherd for his father-in-law's flocks (Exodus 3:1). But in Genesis 46:34, we learn, "Every shepherd is an abomination to the Egyptians." Moses's job was the very thing he'd grown up believing was deplorable. And he wasn't even shepherding his own sheep.

Here we have people in captivity desperate for freedom, and a man who felt like an inadequate failure desperate for purpose. God was about to use both to glorify Himself.

One day, Moses took his father-in-law's flocks to Mount Horeb, also known as Mount Sinai, where he would later be given the Ten Commandments. He noticed a bush burning. Now, it wasn't uncommon in that area to see bushes burning, but as burning bushes do, they burn up. Not this one.

> *He looked, and behold, the bush was burning, yet it was not consumed. And Moses said, "I will turn aside to see this great sight, why the bush is not burned." When the LORD saw that he turned aside to see, God called to him out of the bush, "Moses, Moses."*

—EXODUS 3:2–4

God again uses repetition to make a point. Even though Moses was an insecure, forgotten shepherd, God had not forgotten him. God knew his name. And God wanted to use him.

> *Then the LORD said, "I have surely seen the affliction of my people who are in Egypt and have heard their cry because of their taskmasters. I know their sufferings, and I have come down to deliver them out of the hand of the Egyptians and to bring them up out of that land to a good and broad land, a land flowing with milk and honey, to the place of the Canaanites, the Hittites, the Amorites, the Perizzites, the Hivites, and the Jebusites. And now, behold, the cry of the people of Israel has come to me, and I have also seen the oppression with which the Egyptians oppress them. Come, I will send you to Pharaoh that you may bring my people, the children of Israel, out of Egypt."*

—EXODUS 3:7–10

Whoa, whoa, hold up. Verse eight says, "I have come down to deliver," and verse ten says, "I will send you." If God came down to rescue the Hebrews, why did He need Moses?

In the *Devotional Commentary on Exodus*, F. B. Meyer says:

Why summon a shepherd, a lonely and unbefriended man, a man who has already failed once, and from whom the passing years have stolen his manhood's prime, to work out with painful elaboration, and through a series of bewildering disappointments, the purposed emancipation?

Wouldn't it just be easier and, good gracious, so much faster for the Almighty to come down and speak deliverance over His people? Signed. Sealed. Delivered. Done.

At this unexpected call from God, Moses replied, "Who am I that I should go to Pharaoh and bring the children of Israel out of Egypt?" (Exodus 3:11).

But as we will see, God loves to use ordinary people to fulfill His plan and glorify His name. For *His* fame, not ours.

Moses asked, "Who am I?"

So God replied to Moses, "But I will be with you" (v. 12). Why didn't God answer Moses's question? Come on, now. Moses didn't ask, "Who's coming with me?" Moses asked, "Who am I?"

The answer Moses received was not, by any stretch of the imagination, an assurance of who he was. Moses didn't get an "I'll tell you who you are, Moses. You are perfect. You are called. You are talented. You are Mine. You are adequate. You got this, buddy."

But *here*, who Moses *is*, is not the question God wants to answer. But rather, Who is *with* Moses to get the job done.

Moses asked, "Who am I?" implying his complete inadequacy. God replied, "I will be with you" implying His complete adequacy.

Meyer continues:

Throughout the entire scheme of Divine government, we meet with the principle of mediation. God ever speaks to men, and works for them, through the instrumentality of men. Chosen agents are called into the inner circle, to catch the Divine thought and mirror the Divine character, and then sent back to their fellows, to cause them to partake.

It was intentional on the part of God to let Moses know that it was God who was going to have the power and authority to do this awesome deliverance, not Moses himself. It's as if He's saying, "Yep, you can't do this by yourself, Moses. You can't bring the people out of Egypt by yourself." Or, "You can't write this book on your own, Lisa." Or, dear reader, "You can't fulfill what I'm asking you to do by yourself. *But*. I. Will. Be. With. You."

When God calls me into action, I must not rely on who I am or who I think I am not but on who God is and that He is *with* me and *fully* adequate to do everything through me that He has called me to do. And when He does it through me, He makes Himself famous.

❋ Taking the Job ❋

I knew I had booked the job to write the proposal for this book. But after giving God all the excuses, fueled by my inadequacy, to not write it, I finally conceded. I promised Him I would write when summer began.

As the summer set in, Markus and the kids headed to camp for a week. So that first morning, I lay facedown on the floor in my bedroom and prayed.

"Lord, I have no idea what I'm doing, and that's no surprise to You. And You know I'm scared because I have no idea what's coming. But would You remove all the roadblocks? Would You break down all the obstacles that stand in the way of me getting this proposal completed? Would You remove the barriers of self-doubt and interruptions that will distract me? Eliminate anything that will keep this proposal from getting to the publisher it needs to get to. Would You move me out of Your way? I give my time and my mind to You. I give my heart and my soul and any creativity that I have to You. Use me to write this book, though I still think You're crazy to ask me. Make Yourself famous, and use me to do it."

I came out of my room to my iPad, which lit up with a text message.

The text was from my friend, Arica, who prayed for me as I began this journey. Her text read, *Lisa, I asked the Lord to show me a verse this morning as you start your proposal that would encourage you and meet you right where you are. Here's the verse He led me to.*

I will march out ahead of you. I will make the mountains level. I will break down bronze gates. I will cut through their heavy iron bars. I will give you treasures that are hidden away. I will give you riches that are stored up in secret places. Then you will know that I am the LORD. I am the God of Israel. *I am sending for you by name.*

—ISAIAH 45:2–3 NIrV *(author's emphasis)*

I wept like a baby knowing God gave these verses to me to tell me that He was absolutely adequate, and He would show Himself off through me.

As I reflect back on that time, I know the Lord was guiding each moment of my writing. This time has stretched and challenged me, but I felt His presence, nearness, and His "with me" the entire time.

God showed Himself faithful to remove obstacles over and over again as He brought me a publisher.

And even as I sit at my computer and type right now, I have to remind myself of His promise to me in Isaiah 45. Because I often think like television comedy writer, Louis C. K., who said on the 2015 Emmys, "The hardest part of writing anything is that you have to have ideas. And every time that you have an idea, you feel completely sure that that was your last one."

But as I have felt the presence of God throughout this entire book process, so I believe He will give me the next idea. And He will write the rest of this book, amazingly, through little ol' inadequate me.

When it came to *Chasing Famous*, the Lord said to my "Who am I?" question, "I will be with you. I will do it. Through you. All for My glory."

God's call is seldom easy. That's because His call requires Him. And so we are never in a more perfect place to live out our calling than when we feel completely inadequate.

So how about you? What is God calling you to do? What job has He booked you for, but you feel inadequate to do? Are you willing to replace your feelings of inadequacy with the adequacy of God? Are you willing to believe God? What do you need to do to move forward? Sister, what do you need to do?

May we be women who give our feelings of inadequacy to God. May we replace our inadequacies with Him. May we tell Him, "Whatever You want to do through me, I am willing. I die to myself and replace all of me with You. So do big things through me, God. Show Yourself off and use me to do it."

Questions to Consider:

» What is God calling you to do?

» Do you feel inadequate to do it?

» What's holding you back? Why?

» What might it look like for you to replace your feelings of inadequacy with the adequacy of God?

On Hold

On hold: A casting director will put [an actor] "on hold" when [they] are wanted by the client for the job but not formally hired yet. [The actor] may not take other jobs that would conflict with the production dates during this time. —Acting Studio Chicago

Talent agents Suzanne Horne and Gillian DeGennaro with The Horne Agency in Dallas define the commercial audition process as follows: "The agent submits the actor's headshot and résumé to the casting director, hired by the production company, based on a 'character breakdown' describing the actors needed for the project. The casting director looks over all the actors submitted and narrows down the choices he or she would like to audition for the project. If the actor is selected to be seen, their agent will send them information about the scope of the job. This will include: the name of the project, audition date and time, callback dates, wardrobe fitting date, shoot dates, character description, script (if there is one), and the rate of pay.

"After the audition, the casting director sends the videotaped auditions to the client (production company, ad agency, etc.). They will review the tapes and pare down their top choices for a callback session. These callbacks are usually a couple of days after the initial audition. After the callback, if the clients have interest in a particular actor, they will call the actor's agent and put the actor 'on hold' while they review the final actors under consideration for the role. An actor must let their agent know if there are any conflicts that have developed that would prevent the actor from accepting the job if they are selected. In another day or two, the actor is notified if they are either released (not hired) or booked (hired)."

The commercial business almost always runs this way. But there are times when a few hiccups occur. I once booked a commercial, and we were getting close to the night of the shoot when unforeseen circumstances kept the clients from being available like they thought they would be, and they had to cancel the shoot date. I was put back on hold. Luckily for me, I was paid for the booked night, but I wasn't sure if I would ever get to film the project.

And like this commercial, when booked by God to do something for Him, I may get really close to the big shoot date of doing what He's prepared for me to do. But often I don't feel ready, and I will put myself back on hold. Why? Because the unforeseen circumstance—otherwise known as the inner or external voices of doubt—throw the brakes on my forward momentum. I may be very passionate and willing, but when those voices start to throw fear my way, it's easy to agree with them and second-guess why God would even cast me.

Recently I joined the stage with a popular women's speaker and author. She was to give the keynote talk for the conference, and I was to perform a spoken-word piece I wrote (also known as chapter 1 of this book). A spoken word is a poem that is read or recited using rhythmic voice inflection, creative phrasing, and wordplay to communicate a powerful message. About an hour before the conference, the speaker asked me what my spoken word was about. After I told her, she responded, "Are you kidding me? That is the exact message God gave me to share with the audience after your spoken word."

I was amazed that God had given the same message to two people in two different ways. But I was even more amazed that *I* was one of those people. The voice of the enemy spoke doubt into my heart. I said to the Lord, "Why would You give *me* the same message You gave to someone so popu—." But before I could finish my thought, the Lord said to my heart, "Why *not* you?"

After I wrote the proposal to *Chasing Famous*, I took it to a speaker and writer's conference to pitch it to publishers. While at the conference, I heard three of the main speakers and one breakout speaker mention that our job in life is to "make God famous." I was floored that God said the same thing to me that He was saying to these speakers who reach hundreds of thousands of people with their conferences, books, and blogs. Does God really need me to proclaim His fame when there are others more qualified and with a larger audience? *I'm just a—.* Again, He silenced the enemy with His response. "Lisa, I speak My truths to whoever will communicate them. No matter the size of their platform."

Do you ever do this to yourself? Wonder why you would be used by God? Do you ever think, "I'm just a mom, just a twentysomething, thirtysomething, fortysomething, fiftysomething, etc., just a this, just a that." Blah, blah. If we're not careful, this thinking will paralyze us and keep us from doing what God has called us to do.

We may be passionate about what God's called us to and very willing to do it, but when we look at the scope of the task He's given us to accomplish, we shrink at the thought and think, *Nah, not me.* We think the world-changing business should go to someone else. We allow the voice of the enemy and the voices of others to silence us and put us back on hold.

The Bible shows us stories of people who were given God-sized tasks, and to look at them, their lives didn't seem all that exciting. But in the hands of God, they became trumpets of His instruction and fame. I find comfort in these folks and maybe even a little courage.

Abraham was just a worn-out old man, but in the hands of God, he became the father of God's great nation, even at the age of 100.

Gideon was just a second-guessing solider, but in the hands of God, he defeated 120,000 men with only 300 fighters.

Rahab was just a prostitute, but in the hands of God, she became the many-great-grandmother of Jesus Christ.

The disciples were just regular Joes, but in the hands of God, they healed the sick and cast out demons in Jesus' name.

We may have a desire to do much for God, but we think, *I'm just (fill in the blank).* The opinions of others or the inner doubting voice keep us from allowing God to work mightily through us for His glory.

Let's examine another unsuspecting character who others thought that was *just*. Once God got a hold of him, He changed his world.

* You Are Not Able *

David was the youngest of eight brothers. The oldest three went to battle with King Saul against their enemy, the Philistines. David was an armor bearer, a servant, to King Saul, and he went back and forth from Saul's side to Bethlehem, where he took care of his father's sheep. One day his dad asked him to take food to his brothers on the battlefront and then come back home and let him know how the strapping lads were doing. David trekked to the frontlines but found no one fighting. The battle—dead as a doornail. The soldiers—scared stiff.

For 40 days, the Philistines presented a nine-foot-tall giant named Goliath. Goliath threw threats around and promised to defeat any Israelite who approached him. And though King Saul promised lots of reward to the man who defeated Goliath, not even the strongest Israeli military warrior was willing to approach this guy.

But the Lord put within David a passion and a disgust when he saw Goliath "defying the armies of the living God." And David said he would be the one to kill this "uncircumcised Philistine" (1 Samuel 17:26). David saw that no one else was stepping up, but the job needed to be done. And he said, "I am that somebody."

But David was *just* a kid. *Just* a shepherd. *Just* a water boy. He was probably short and skinny and completely ill-equipped to fight a giant who couldn't even fit in my living room. In the eyes of others, he was a nobody. But he was the only somebody who was willing to fight Goliath.

What happens when the majority is fearful and unwilling to do something that an underdog offers to do instead? The majority becomes defensive and embarrassed. I assume this fueled David's brother, Eliab, to respond to David's bravery and willingness the way he did.

{ *Now Eliab his eldest brother heard when he spoke to the men. And Eliab's anger was kindled against David, and he said, "Why have you come down? And with whom have you left those few sheep in the wilderness? I know your presumption and the evil of your heart, for you have come down to see the battle."* }

—1 SAMUEL 17:28 *(author's emphasis)*

Eliab saw Samuel anoint David to be the future king of Israel. No doubt Eliab was jealous, and this emotion also drove his response to David. But David doesn't allow his older brother's words to discourage him, "What have I done now? Was it not but a word?" (v. 29). A message gets back to King Saul, who is also hiding from Goliath, that unsuspecting David has agreed to kill the giant. And now he too tries to discourage the willing God follower.

{ You are not able *to go against this Philistine to fight with him, for you are but a youth, and he has been a man of war from his youth.* }

—v. 33 *(author's emphasis)*

But David's confidence is not rattled. He remembers God's past faithfulness. And this fuels his passion to do what God's asking him to do.

{ *But David said to Saul, "Your servant used to keep sheep for his father. And when there came a lion, or a bear, and took a lamb from the flock, I went after him and struck him and delivered it out of his mouth. And if he arose against me, I caught him by his beard and struck him and killed him. Your servant has struck down both lions and bears, and this uncircumcised Philistine shall be like one of them, for he has defied the armies of the living God." And David said, "The* LORD *who delivered me from the paw of the lion and from the paw of the bear will deliver me from the hand of this Philistine." And Saul said to David, "Go, and the* LORD *be with you!"* }

—vv. 34–37

The fact that David referred to God as "the living God" showed David's conviction that Yahweh was still the same One who could defeat this enemy as He had defeated enemies in the past.

David hadn't forgotten how God protected him in the past, and his confidence convinced Saul to release David to fight Goliath. He put on David his own armor, helmet, and sword. But Saul's war clothes were way too big for little David. So David took them off.

Instead, he gathered five smooth stones he found by a stream and took his sling to fight the giant.

This sling was not a child's toy but an ancient offensive weapon used in war. Shepherds also used them in leadership of their sheep. These slings were handmade out of a long, thin strip of leather with a pouch in the middle. Particularly talented warriors wielded their slingshots to accurately propel small objects hundreds of feet at very high speeds.

But this little boy and his sling didn't faze Goliath. And now it's Goliath's turn to voice his doubts about David's ability to take him out.

And when the Philistine looked and saw David, he disdained him, for he was but a youth, *ruddy and handsome in appearance. And the Philistine said to David, "Am I a dog, that you come to me with sticks?" And the Philistine cursed David by his gods.*

—1 SAMUEL 17:42–43 *(author's emphasis)*

But David didn't allow any of the doubting voices or opinions to silence the voice of Truth. What pushed David forward, despite the doubters, was his passionate jealously for the reputation of God.

This day the LORD will deliver you into my hand, and I will strike you down and cut off your head. And I will give the dead bodies of the host of the Philistines this day to the birds of the air and to the wild beasts of the earth, that all the earth may know that there is a God in Israel, *and that all this assembly may know that the LORD saves not with sword and spear. For the battle is the LORD's, and he will give you into our hand.*

—1 SAMUEL 17:46–47 *(author's emphasis)*

David knew "the LORD sees not as man sees: man looks on the outward appearance, but the LORD looks on the heart" (1 Samuel 16:7). God will use anyone, even if they are just a (fill in the blank). No matter their size, shape, color, marital status, past failed efforts, or successful attempts. God doesn't care about using people who "look the part" but those who are ready to make Him famous.

In the eyes of man, there was nothing special about David. But to God, David was extraordinary, not because God made him better than anyone else but because God made him. God creates all people with the ability to glorify Him. David was unique because he refused to let anything or anyone stand in the way of what God wanted him to do.

What God saw was a young kid who loved Him. When He searched for someone who would glorify His name, He saw David, a man after His own heart (1 Samuel 13:14). He was passionate and willing. When we, like David, are passionately jealous for the reputation of God through us, God will open up doors no giant can close.

It's easy to look at David and think, *David had an extraordinary faith in God. Fear and the doubting voices of others couldn't penetrate his heart. No wonder he had the confidence he did.* But later in his life David experienced great fear and was not immune from doubt or pain. David pens his own struggles throughout the Book of Psalms.

> *My heart is in anguish within me; the terrors of death have fallen upon me. Fear and trembling come upon me, and horror overwhelms me.*
>
> —PSALM 55:4–5

We see how the words of man affect him.

> *But I am a worm and not a man, scorned by mankind and despised by the people. All who see me mock me; they make mouths at me; they wag their heads.*
>
> —PSALM 22:6–7

But he knew God was the One to call on when he struggled.

> *Out of my distress I called on the LORD; the LORD answered me and set me free.*
>
> —PSALM 118:5

He trusted God to deliver him when the voices of others were louder than God's.

{ *He rescued me from my strong enemy and from those who hated me, for they were too mighty for me. They confronted me in the day of my calamity, but the LORD was my support. He brought me out into a broad place; he rescued me, because he delighted in me.* }

—PSALM 18:17–19

David slung a single stone toward Goliath, and God directed the stone directly into the giant's forehead. Some scholars suggest that this made Goliath pass out, causing him to fall forward and hit the ground, at which point David ran over to the giant and killed him by cutting off his head.

{ *When the Philistines saw their champion was dead, they fled.* }

—1 SAMUEL 17:51

The Israelite army chased the freaked-out Philistines and plundered their camp.

And who got the glory? David? Yeah, right. God did. And David's promise to Goliath in 1 Samuel 17:46 came true: "all the earth may know that there is a God in Israel."

The crazy thing about this story is that there was a huge task to be done, and it looked like David would fail. I mean, weren't there more qualified and skilled people? People who had done this before and had more bravery? Everyone could see it. But clearly, God hadn't used those people and wasn't planning on it. He wanted to use someone that no one expected and do something that no one could do. No one, that is, except God.

* Why Not You? *

This is what I believe God loves to do: use people who tell themselves or have been told by others "you are not able." And I love that we get to respond, "No, I am not, but God is. And He will make Himself famous through me."

So why not you? What are you passionate about and willing to do but, as you look around, you see more qualified people to do it? What is it that people tell you, "There's no way you can do that." What giant towers over you and seems impossible to defeat?

David was *just* a teenage shepherd, but in the hands of God, he defeated Goliath, became the greatest king of Israel, and the many-great-grandfather of Jesus Christ.

You've "booked the job." Don't put yourself back "on hold."

God isn't looking for someone worthy but someone willing. Go on. I dare you to step out and make God famous.

Imagine God's fame as you fill in the blanks.

(Your name) _____ is just _____ .

But in the hands of God will _____

_____ .

Questions to Consider:

» What are you passionate about doing for the glory of God? Are you doing it?

» Do you see others doing what you'd love to do? If so, how do you feel as you watch them? Do you feel defeated? Relieved? Jealous like Eliab?

» If you're not doing what God's called you to do, why haven't you stepped forward to do it? Are the negative voices of others paralyzing you? Do you think the task is for someone more qualified? Are you afraid to fail? Are you worried about what others will think of you?

» What do you think would happen if you did move forward?

» Do you think your moving forward would glorify God? Why?

12

Wait for Your Cue

Waiting on [God] exercises your gift of grace and tests your faith. Therefore continue to wait in hope, for although the promise may linger, it will never come too late.
—Charles Spurgeon

Waiting for your cue is very important in any scene. If an actor comes onto the stage or into view of the camera too late or too early, the moment the director is trying to create for the scene can be ruined for the audience.

I recently did a commercial that was filmed in one shot—meaning the camera started rolling and continued rolling for the entire 30 second spot. No stops.

My cue to begin the scene was when, from my peripheral vision, I saw the camera rise to my face. Then I checked off an item on my to-do list. The camera passed me, I followed it. I squeezed into the tight space between the camera operator and a Christmas tree, high-fived my "son," went off camera, caught a Christmas present in the air (thrown to me by the assistant director), and then sat down on the chair by the fireplace just in time for the camera to pass by me while I was opening the present. The timing had to be perfect. The camera operator, me, the dad, the kid, and even a dog, had to wait for our cues and hit our marks perfectly. If not, we started over. You can imagine it was a very nerve-wracking shoot. But waiting for our cues made for a great commercial.

God sometimes asks us to wait for our cue too. Maybe you have figured out your gifts and talents and have a good idea of how God could use them. But each time you go to open the door to use your gifts, it's locked, and you're frustrated to no end. He's asked you to wait, but why?

* Why Do I Have to Wait? *

I knew God gave me the gifts of speaking and teaching, but I felt tied down to my job at the time. Each day I woke up and wondered, *Is today the day that God will call me on stage to take my place to communicate His desire to be made famous?* But years went by at this job, and I was still waiting. And waiting. Waiting for my cue.

I was angry and frustrated that I had the job I had and not the job I longed for. So the quality of my work suffered as I allowed bitterness to settle into my heart. It wasn't pretty.

Maybe, like me, you know your gifts and talents and have a good idea of how God could use them. Maybe God's gifted you to speak and teach, to run a nonprofit, or to care for the disabled. And you know that when released to use your gifts, you will reflect His image and His glory to anyone who will pay attention. You think you're ready, so you wonder, *Why isn't God using me right now? He's given me the gift and the desire, but not the opportunity.*

As a result, maybe your work or your relationships suffer. Your attitude toward what you're doing now has grown cold.

You know you should wait well, but how do we wait well when we're waiting for our cue?

Turns out, there are a couple guys in Scripture who were called by God but had to wait years for Him to call them to the stage.

* A Shepherd *

David was anointed by Samuel to be king over Israel when he was just 15 years old. But he didn't take the throne until he was 37. When Samuel came to him, he was a humble shepherd (1 Samuel 16:11). After his anointing, his job was to play the lyre for Saul, the current king of Israel, and, as we saw in chapter 11, be his armor bearer—a personal assistant.

David knew he wouldn't always be a mere shepherd and servant. He knew God had called him to lead the people of Israel. Yet, unlike me, David waited well. He wasn't distracted by the fact that he was not king yet. His work didn't suffer, and he didn't complain. He was faithful in the job he had as evidenced when Saul said to David's dad, Jesse, "Let David remain in my service for he has found favor in my sight" (1 Samuel 16:22).

* A Servant *

Even Jesus had to wait 33 years for His Father to open up the door to what He was called to do. And though Jesus dreaded the physical, spiritual, and emotional pain of His Crucifixion, He looked with longing to the Cross, knowing you and I were at stake. He waited on the perfect timing of God. He didn't rush or question Him. And while He waited, He was faithful.

* Faithful in the Now *

After yet another evening of "couch complaining" about my job and wondering why God hadn't released me yet, my wise husband said, "Why would God want to release you to do what He's gifted you to do if you can't even be faithful in what you're doing right now? He's not opening up doors for you to speak. So if I were you, I'd be grateful for the job you have and do it well."

In my head I thought, *Just stop, Markus. Stop being discerning and sensitive to the Holy Spirit. Stop being obedient to tell me what I need to hear. Ugh.*

Don't you hate it when people who love the Lord and love you speak sensibly to you? I hope you can smell my sarcasm.

Markus was right.

Why in the world would God call me—or you—to do big things for His name and fame if we can't even be faithful with the things He's placed before us right now? If I'm not going to be grateful or work hard in the small task, I won't in the big task either. It's an attitude thing.

It's like my kiddo asking me for a new bike when he leaves his old one out in the rain to rust all the time, even when I've told him over and over again to put it in the garage. Why would I give him a new one? I'd want him to show himself and me that he respects and cares for what I've given him. If I want God to open up doors, I need to be grateful for where I am and faithful to make Him famous there. If God is waiting on me, I don't want to give Him any reason to wait any longer.

But there are things I can do while I wait. I can wipe away any preconceived ideas of what "success" with my calling looks like and know that my idea of success and God's idea of success in using my gifts could be totally opposite. And I can also take advantage of situations of the "now" and look for opportunities to use my gifts and talents that relate to what God has called me to do.

* You Can Always Choose Your Attitude *

"You can always choose your attitude," my mom likes to say. So I decided to choose a better one about not having as many opportunities to speak as I would like. I never understood why God wasn't allowing me to teach more, but I understood that being angry wouldn't change anything. I decided to take advantage of the times I had in front of the people I did lead. I utilized my meetings at work to teach and cast vision. I included bits of teaching in the emails I sent to those I led to encourage them. I saw my blog as an opportunity to teach as well. I decided to be grateful for where I was and pray God would use me there instead of wishing I were somewhere else.

As a result, my anger subsided, my work was more productive, and I found a new energy. I believed the best of God and trusted He had perfect timing. I just had to wait for my cue.

Like a director of a production or shoot, God sees the big picture and understands how the entire scene needs to operate for ultimate effectiveness. So we have to wait for our cue if we want the scene to be the best it can be.

We tend to think, *Now!* as soon as we get a calling. But we don't consider what else may be at stake.

* God's Omniscience *

God's people had been enslaved in Egypt for hundreds of years. At the age of 40, God placed within Moses a desire to see his people free. But it wasn't yet God's time for Moses to move forward with the call to save his people. What moved God into action to use Moses? Something else that had nothing to do with Moses.

> During those many days the king of Egypt died, and the people of Israel groaned because of their slavery and cried out for help. Their cry for rescue from slavery came up to God. And God heard their groaning, and God remembered his covenant with Abraham, with Isaac, and with Jacob. God saw the people of Israel—and God knew*.
>
> —EXODUS 2:23–25

*means "had concern for" in Hebrew

In the notes of my ESV Study Bible, it says anytime we see the word "remember" in regard to God "remembering" someone or His covenant with that person in the Old Testament, it means that God is about to go into action on someone's behalf.

Did you see that the prayer of the people is what moved the heart of God into action? It wasn't Moses saying, "God, I'm ready. I'm sick of my boring job as a shepherd in Midian. I'm not getting any younger here, let's go." What moved God into action was not Moses's readiness but Israel's cry. Moses isn't even mentioned in this passage. It appears that God opening the door for Moses to live into his calling had less to do with Moses and everything to do with Israel's prayers.

God's timing was also affected by His understanding of the future. Pharaoh would release the slaves the morning after the Jews celebrated their first annual Passover meal of the sacrificial lamb. God knew Jesus' death on the Cross would replace this yearly celebration, and Jesus Himself would be the final, one-time substitute for the offering. His death had to time out perfectly 1,500 years later with the celebration of the Passover in Jerusalem. As He saw the mistreatment of His people, God may have wanted to free the slaves before He did, but His omniscient understanding of the future kept Him from moving prematurely.

What if God's timing in my life has less to do with me and more to do with His divine plan? Why would I want to rush God?

* An Elephant, Four Blind Men, and a King *

I once heard a parable about an elephant, four blind men, and a king. The king gathered the blind men and, not telling them what the animal was, asked them to touch the creature and describe what they "saw." The one who touched the side of the elephant said it was like a wall. The one who touched the leg said the elephant was like a tree trunk. The one who touched the end of the elephant's tail said it was like a broom. The one who touched the trunk said the elephant was like a hose. Based on what they touched, each blind man thought they were correct and the others were wrong. But the king, who could see the animal in its entirety, said, "You are all incorrect. You only understand the little section in front of you, but I can see the animal in its entirety." They could only "see" in part. They could not grasp the totality of the beast.

So it is with our understanding of God's timing. I only "see" the small part in front of me. I won't always know why God makes me wait. But I know He sees the entire picture. And while I wait for God to free me to share my gifts with the world, I want to wait for my cue and be faithful wherever He has me.

Is my deep desire to reflect the glory of God, or is it to do it in the way, place, timing, and method that I think it should be done?

Do I trust God—really trust Him? Do I have confidence that God knows better than me? Do I believe God sees the big picture while I only see the trunk or the end of the tail?

God has given you and me gifts and talents to be used for His glory and fame. He wants for us to use them more than we do. But sometimes He's waiting on us. Sometimes He's waiting on someone or something else. When we are asked to wait for our cue, we must remember to do our current task well and see how we could use the gifts given to us in small ways right now. His perfect timing so often affects more than just you and me. God wants us, and sometimes waits on us, to patiently rely on His perfect timing for our lives. To place Him right where He belongs—on the throne of our lives and to trust Him. May we not miss the opportunity to be used by God where we are because we're so consumed with a desire to be used by God where we're not.

Waiting! Yes, waiting! Still waiting!

The Master will not be late:

Since He knows that I am waiting

For Him to unlatch the gate.

—J. Danson Smith

Questions to Consider:

» Is God asking you to wait on His timing to use the gifts He's given you? If so, how?

» How does this make you feel?

» If you don't feel that God is using you to your full potential yet, how can you use the gifts He's given you now?

» Imagine for a moment what God might be waiting on before He fully releases you. Could He be waiting on you? Why? Could He be waiting on someone or something else? Who? What?

» What are some situations God has you in right now where He might want to use you more?

» Pray you will have the patience to *truly* give Him your wait.

SECTION 3:

YOUR EVERY DAY FOR THE EMINENCE OF GOD

In addition to using our stories and our talents for His glory, God wants to use us in our everyday, regular lives to radiate His splendor. If I'm honest with you, I think sometimes it's easier to make God famous in the "big" things like our testimonies and talents than in the ho-hum of the every day—in the little things that don't get acknowledged by the people we love and serve. But God sees us. He sees our discipline and resolve to glorify Him in the way we make choices, both externally and internally, even if no one else does. In these everyday moments, will we beat down our flesh so the Holy Spirit can rise up within us and make Himself famous?

13

The Aside

{ *Do not let any unwholesome talk come out of your mouths, but only what is helpful for building others up according to their needs, that it may benefit those who listen.* }

—EPHESIANS 4:29 NIV

Asides are a fabulous way of bringing the audience into the story. The audience feels a part of what's going on, often hearing the true opinions of the character speaking to them. Asides cause the audience to "lean in" so they don't miss what the character is saying. And asides are often witty and sarcastic. Famous playwrights like William Shakespeare, Anton Chekhov, and Arthur Miller used asides to draw their audiences close.

A more modern-day example of great asides is Jim's unspoken ones to the camera in the sitcom, *The Office.* Or do any of you remember getting pre-teen butterflies when Zack on *Saved by the Bell* would turn to the camera and tell us his thoughts? I would've given anything to be Kelly Kapowski when I was 12 years old. In all asides, the other characters never hear the actor's thoughts to the audience or see them happening. The character's comments to those on the other side of the camera or in the audience always express true, raw feelings about people or situations in that moment. In an aside, a character may be mistaken, but he or she is never dishonest.

Asides offer emotional insight or facts to help move a story along. But most importantly, asides are an opportunity for the character to candidly gossip to their captivated audience.

* Justifying Asides *

I make gossip asides to my husband . . . a lot. I may not let other people know how I feel about them, but I sure am quick to tell Markus my honest thoughts. My asides often happen after the kids go to bed, and we're swapping stories of our day while sitting on the couch. And my asides fall out of my mouth uninhibited.

Talking with him is like talking to myself. I even try to justify gossiping to him because I think, *Aw, it's no big deal, he's like my second skin. And he won't tell anyone. And it will feel good to have someone else share in my "sufferings."* But when I gossip to Markus, I'm sure to affect his opinion of the person I'm talking about. And even add kindling to the fire of frustration already in my heart.

Do you struggle with this? Maybe like me, you justify gossip to your husband or friend. Or maybe there's a situation at work or church and you and your co-workers or your small group members gather around, and, because everyone is aware of the situation, it feels warranted to talk about it. When you know that if that person were standing right there, they'd be horrified. The Holy Spirit may even persuade us to stay silent, but we will ignore Him for the sake of releasing our frustrations.

There's something that feels good about getting our emotions out of our minds and hearts and landing them on someone else. Other times we want a wrong righted, and we feel vindicated talking about how hurt we are. And still other times we feel insecure, and putting someone down makes us feel better about ourselves. But "asides" are a far cry from making God famous. Because gossip is always all about me.

This is why taming the tongue is one of the hardest things for us. But if we don't slow down and consider the power of our tongue, we will do long-standing damage that we might not have considered when we quickly unleashed our thoughts.

When I gossip despite the nagging Holy Spirit telling me not to, I'm exercising a complete lack of self-discipline. Proverbs 17:28 (NIV) says, "Even fools are thought wise if they keep silent, and discerning if they hold their tongue."

But speaking negatively is so frequent, habitual, and common-place, I quickly forget how icky and opposite it is from reflecting the image of God. Because when I gossip, I'm at the front of the stage, like an actor about to unleash an aside, waiting for the audience to listen.

So how do I gather the discipline to stop?

* Stop. Think. Do what's right. *

I once heard a couple share a story of how they were trying to help their son have self-control. They would say to him, "Stop, think, do what's right." And each word had a hand motion. For "stop" he would throw his palm in front of him, making a "Stop" motion—imagine The Supremes singing "Stop! In the Name of Love." For "think" he would point to his temple. And for "do what's right" he would do the "thumbs up" sign. Stop, think, do what's right.

The purpose of this exercise was to get him to slow down and think before acting on a bad choice.

Though a child's exercise, it's a good one for adults too, with or without hand motions. The key to taming the tongue is slowing down long enough to give myself a chance to listen to the Holy Spirit before I open my mouth. And then exercising the self-discipline to keep my mouth shut.

* The Tongue Ain't No Joke *

God knows how difficult it is to keep a tight rein on what we say. James tell us that the tongue ain't no joke.

For we all stumble in many ways. And if anyone does not stumble in what he says, he is a perfect man, able also to bridle his whole body. If we put bits into the mouths of horses so that they obey us, we guide their whole bodies as well. Look at the ships also: though they are so large and are driven by strong winds, they are guided by a very small rudder wherever the will of the pilot directs. So also the tongue is a small member, yet it boasts of great things. . . . For every kind of beast and bird, of reptile and sea creature, can be tamed and has been tamed by mankind, but no human being can tame the tongue. It is a restless evil, full of deadly poison.

—JAMES 3:2–5, 7–8

James is saying that the small bridle can control the large horse, and the small rudder can control an even larger ship. And the tongue is also small compared to the rest of the body. But unlike the bridle and the rudder, controlled by man, man cannot discipline the tongue. James is implying that only God can discipline the tongue. But this is doable because God's Spirit lives within us and has given us all we need to act as He wants us to.

A horse, if he does not see his rider as in full authority over him, will not allow the small bridle to control him. So our tongues have to be in full submission to God to allow Him to master them.

But the fruit of the Spirit is love, joy, peace, patience, kindness, goodness, faithfulness, gentleness, self-control; against such things there is no law.

—GALATIANS 5:22–23

We've all been given the ability to have self-discipline—"God's power has given us everything we need to lead a godly life" (2 Peter 1:3 NIrV)—we just need to exercise it.

The authors of Proverbs wrote the book so we could "know wisdom and instruction" (Proverbs 1:2). With my tongue I glorify God, and with my tongue I defame Him.

So it's not surprising that Proverbs has a lot to say about our speech.

{ *A gossip betrays a confidence, but a trustworthy person keeps a secret.* }

—PROVERBS 11:13 NIV

{ *The words of the reckless pierce like swords, but the tongue of the wise brings healing.* }

—PROVERBS 12:18 NIV

{ *A perverse person stirs up conflict, and a gossip separates close friends.* }

—PROVERBS 16:28 NIV

{ *Those who guard their mouths and their tongues keep themselves from calamity.* }

—PROVERBS 21:23 NIV

When I want to gossip about someone, it's because I don't see him or her as God does. If I had God's view of them, despite the pain or frustration they may have caused me, I would be quick to find their positive qualities, seeing that I'm no better than they are. Gossip puts me above someone because I see them as less than me. And this posture of my heart keeps me center stage instead of God.

The other day, I wanted to unleash my frustrations about someone to my husband. Because Markus was acquainted with this person and their behavior, I knew he would share my anger, and our conversation would stoke this fire and justify my bad feelings. I couldn't wait until Markus got home. And when I heard the garage door open, I grew disgustingly excited. But the Holy Spirit stopped me. I analyzed and thought about my motives. I knew the only reason I would talk with Markus about this was to encourage negative thoughts about this person. And then I did what was right. As hard as it was, I didn't say anything to Markus, even though I really, *like really, really* wanted to. And I knew I had obeyed God.

I wish my obedience made my thoughts go away, like when I

vacuum the grass out of my minivan after a week of soccer and base-ball practice. But my icky thoughts stick. So I have to constantly pray for a heart to see others as God does. I have to work to assume the best of that person, understanding that there's always a "why" for their actions. And usually the "why" is because of pain. People act the way they do, not because they *want* to hurt me or others, but because they themselves are hurting or are longing to satisfy an unmet need. When I keep this perspective, as hard as it is, my heart breaks for them, I feel empathy, and I go to my knees on their behalf instead of running my mouth. And when I see them again, most of the time, my frustration has subsided and I have a compassionate heart for them. At least this is what I'm going for. This is how I want to live.

* Stepping Aside from the Aside *

So how about you? Maybe there's someone in your life right now you are tempted to make an "aside" about. Is it a friend, your children, your husband, a co-worker, a politician, or someone less fortunate than you?

Ask God to give you a heart for that person, to see them as He sees them, to restore your relationship with them, to give you the courage to not add to the conversation of gossip. You can smile and change the subject, talk about their good qualities, or just stay silent. Ask Him to speak loudly to you when you are tempted to gossip. And to give you the courage to stop, think, and do what's right.

There will be times when it's important to talk with our husbands, a close family member, or friend about how we feel about a person who's hurt us. We may need their wisdom about how to handle the situation and move forward or how to have a discussion with the person who's hurt us to bring the relationship back into balance. But we must analyze our motives—only we know the true intentions of our hearts. Are we honestly trying to solve the problem? Or are we masking gossip?

We will loudly make God famous when we choose to have self-control and not participate in the asides, though the script running through our heads may call for them. Our self-control will keep us away from the front of the stage, and God there instead, as we stop, think, and do what's right.

Questions to Consider:

» Who are you most tempted to talk about *(go ahead, tell me, tell me!)*?

» Why do you feel the need to talk about them?

» Do you think you should stop gossiping about them? Do you think you could control your tongue long enough to "Stop, think, and do what's right"?

» Can you imagine that there might be a "why" for their actions? What could be an unmet need they are trying to satisfy?

» What might it feel like to not gossip?

» How might this change you?

» How might this glorify God in your life?

14

Photoshop

Photoshop: To alter (a digital image) with Photoshop software or other image-editing software especially in a way that distorts reality (as for deliberately deceptive purposes). —*Merriam-Webster's Dictionary*

 You are altogether beautiful, my love; there is no flaw in you.

—SONG OF SOLOMON 4:7

Our bodies, though important, are not everything and they certainly do not define us. The human form is merely a vessel through which a brilliant mind and soul exist. That's *the truly important part of a person. If some women just so happen to have pretty packaging, good for them, but we're moving on.*
—A. Lutes

D o you ever look at a magazine, billboard, or ad on social media and think, *Man, she is perfect—a perfect face and a perfect body.* Do you ever stand in line at the grocery store and stare in disbelief at the lack of flaws you see? That's because those women. Are. Not. Real. They have been altered on a computer through a digital editing software called Photoshop. And the brilliance of the marketing is that though the pictures make you feel horrible about yourself, you want to add the magazine to your grocery cart or click on the ad for more, to see if inside it's offerings lie the key to what they are advertising— perfection.

Vicki Courtney, author of *5 Conversations You Must Have With Your Daughter*, says, "One has to wonder if the primary agenda of the fashion magazines is to create a level of dissatisfaction among their female readers regarding their overall body image in an effort to keep them running back for more and more advice on how to achieve this impossible beauty ideal."

Professional photographer Tim Lynch, who estimates that 99.9 percent of all pictures in an entire magazine are retouched, says, "The Hollywood types have a personal retoucher who does this [retouching] all day long, and they pay them really well. And not one picture is released without their permission. It's just the way they want to be viewed by the world. They want to have this sort of perfection. Which is not possible."

The Dove Foundation did a survey in which 81 percent of women surveyed agreed with the following statement: "Media and advertising set an unrealistic standard of beauty that most women can't ever achieve."

And though we see a standard of beauty few can achieve, we still desperately want to attain it. But it's virtually impossible. So how do we free ourselves from the yoke that links us to this animal of perfection?

As I mentioned in chapter 8, I grew up as a dancer. Spending eight hours a week in front of floor to ceiling mirrors on all four sides of a dance studio in a leotard and tights did nothing for my self-esteem—especially when I went through puberty.

And when I went to college as a theater major and spent what seemed like every waking moment in the arts building, I was surrounded by superskinny dancers who walked from class to class in their dance shorts and midriff baring shirts. As I looked at their bodies, I felt "fat," even though I was far from it. Body conscious, my wardrobe consisted of baggy sweatshirts and pants to hide my figure. I never owned the truth of the fact that what God thinks about me is way more important than anything or anyone who tells me otherwise. My negative view of my body kept me focused inward on myself rather than focused outward to show God off to the world.

And I associated skinny with beauty.

Maybe you do too.

* The New Skinny *

I recently saw a shirt on a rack at a clothing store. It read, "Strong is the new skinny." I immediately thought it was referring to muscle strength and that a physically strong body is now more desirable than a small number on a scale. But as I turned the phrase over in my mind, I thought it also might be communicating that inner strength of mind and heart and confidence are now more desirable than being skinny . . . at least to the person wearing the shirt. Were I to wear the shirt and identify with its meaning, I would translate it, "The new skinny is pushing back lies that tell me I'm anything less than beautiful to God."

 You are altogether beautiful, my love; there is no flaw in you.

—SONG OF SOLOMON 4:7

I think it takes a certain kind of gal to *truly* believe that statement. To *honestly* believe that when it comes to our bodies, there is more to us than being skinny. This would be a new way of living life for many women. A freed-up way of living, actually, that allows *God*—not me—to define who I am.

And yet this is the way God intended it. When God created humans, He said within the Trinity, "Let us make man in our image, after our likeness" (Genesis 1:26). He wasn't suggesting that humans reflect the physical, external appearance of Himself. Rather He was speaking to the internal qualities expressed externally through our words and actions and our dominion over creation. Since God created us in His image, we are a visible representative of His Deity, thus we rule, reign, and live on behalf of and for God to a world that hasn't embraced its identity in Jesus.

* God Sees His Creation, Mankind, as Very Good *

Prior to this point in Genesis 1, God stated that His created works were, "good" (Genesis 1:4, 10, 12, 18, 21, 25). But only *after* God created man and woman, He said that everything He made was *very* good. "And God saw everything that he had made, and behold, it was very good" (Genesis 1:31).

My ESV Study Bible *notes say, "The additional 'behold' invites the readers to imagine seeing creation from God's vantage point."*

Before resting on the seventh day, God took one last grand, sweeping panoramic view of all that He made and, with a big exhale, He knew He created perfection—sky, sun, moon, land, water, plants, creatures, and humans. He looked at us and saw us as complete and not lacking anything or needing change. God had created a world where He could be glorified and the people He placed within it could be representatives of His glory. We were made to be ambassadors to express the fame of God throughout all of creation. Yes, we are very good.

Yet there is always an enemy to good. When Satan heard that God adored His creation, he set out on a mission to change the perception. Because if he can distract us from how good—rather, very good—we are and how extremely good our Father is, then we will quickly become sidetracked from glorifying God. Our focus goes from the external worship of the majesty of God to the internal worship of the perfection of self.

And we do worship ourselves.

Now, women and girls spend hours at the gym and observe calorie-restricted diets as we stand in jealous awe of women who model swimsuits and lingerie. We stand on the scale each morning hoping the number will be lower than yesterday. We stand naked, suck in our stomach, turn sideways, and imagine a body different from what we see in the mirror. We long for our younger bodies, before gravity got ahold of the one staring back at us. We look with disdain at our sagging postbaby selves rather than celebrating that God grew nothing into something under no control of our own. We see stretch marks as a call to cosmetic surgery rather than battle scars leading to the greatest love we may ever know this side of heaven.

And I wonder if God cries. Because we have it all wrong.

He longs for us to see ourselves as He does. But the pull of Satan and the media he uses is often too strong to resist.

✤ The Goal of Media We Pay For ✤

Advertisers show perfect, Photoshopped bodies in order to have us so dissatisfied with our bodies that we will see what they sell as a necessity to our happiness.

The media shows us perfection through Photoshop, and since we can't see the corrections made, what we see with our eyes, we believe as truth.

Photoshop continues to perpetuate our culture's high standard of beauty, and it allows us to see women with no wrinkles, no age spots, no gray hairs, and no cellulite. But I have all of these.

The media tells us—and we tend to agree—that God's standards of perfection aren't really perfection at all and that the Creator of all makes prolific mistakes. It's ludicrous. The God who put the world on its axis and balances planets in the sky, who keeps gravity at just the right strength so we stay put, who placed every hair on your head, who put each pore on your skin, and keeps your heart beating with just a thought—He doesn't make mistakes.

> For you formed my inward parts; you knitted me together in my mother's womb. I praise you, for I am fearfully and wonderfully made. Wonderful are your works; my soul knows it very well. My frame was not hidden from you, when I was being made in secret, intricately woven in the depths of the earth. Your eyes saw my unformed substance; in your book were written, every one of them, the days that were formed for me, when as yet there was none of them.

—PSALM 139:13–16

This God, *this* God, is crazy about you and me, and we have captivated His heart (Song of Solomon 4:9).

* God Doesn't See as Man Sees *

If God were going to create only one thing beautiful in the eyes of mankind, would it not have been His Son? Yet:

> [Jesus] had no form or majesty that we should look at him, and no beauty that we should desire him. He was despised and rejected by men, a man of sorrows and acquainted with grief; as one from whom men hide their faces he was despised, and we esteemed him not.

—ISAIAH 53:2-3

Instead of being externally beautiful, Jesus was obedient to God—the most beautiful thing of all.

> I glorified you on earth, *having accomplished the work that you gave me to do.*

—JOHN 17:4 *(author's emphasis)*

> *I made known to them your name, and I will continue to make it known.*

—v. 26

His perspective on our purpose is not external beauty as far as the world is concerned but people living into their purposes while they are on earth.

If God wanted the world to see and value Jesus like we see and value everything else, He would have made Him beautiful in our eyes, and His entrance into the world would have been glorious, accompanied by worldwide rejoicing. But instead, all of heaven rejoiced because God and His angels knew we didn't need a physically beautiful king. We needed a Savior, and our hearts needed a change. And this is what we are called to present and represent to a world desperately in need of the true beauty of Jesus. And so we, too, have to value what God does.

{ *And when he had removed [Saul], he raised up David to be their king, of whom he testified and said, "I have found in David the son of Jesse a man after my own heart, who will do all my will."* }

−ACTS 13:22

I want God to say that of me, "Lisa is a woman after My own heart; she will do everything I want her to do. She embraces who I've made her to be. She rejects the lies of the enemy that tell her otherwise. She is not concerned with the image she sees in the mirror but is bent on reflecting My image to those who need My message."

* We Must Redefine Beauty for Our World *

The redefinition of beauty starts with you and me.

You and I have the opportunity to recapture the original intent of creation. You have the chance to see yourself as God sees you—*very good*. You have the power to say to Satan, "I refuse to believe you. I instead embrace my job as an image-bearer of God. I am a visible representative of His Deity. The rest of the world and the lie in the mirror may not see me as God does, but they are not my standard or my authority. Get behind me, Satan. I've got a mission to make God famous, and I will no longer allow you to distract me."

What if we started looking away from the Photoshopped images and ignored the lie that tells us we will never measure up? What if we replaced the lie with truth that says we were made on purpose for a purpose and that purpose has nothing to do with the size of our jeans?

What if we no longer went to the gym because we felt guilty for eating a second dessert but in order to make our bodies strong so we have more energy to offer to others and glorify God as a result?

Imagine, instead of trying to perfect our already decaying body, we lived for the fame of God and helping His world.

Imagine how this would change our children's view of women and their view of themselves.

Imagine how it would free us up to live fully into our God-given purpose because we are no longer blown off course.

Imagine how it would disband Satan.

May we see ourselves from God's vantage point: "Behold, you are beautiful, my love, behold, you are beautiful!" (Song of Solomon 4:1).

And after hundreds of years of bondage in this area, may we shake off the shackles and go back to the beginning of creation where a woman stood naked and rejoiced at God's creation (Genesis 2:25). May we live freed up, and may our resolve to see ourselves as the image bearers of God be the new skinny.

Questions to Consider:

» What was your perception of your body growing up?

» How has your perception changed? Stayed the same?

» Do you think you could ever embrace and believe, without limitations, how God views you? "You are altogether beautiful, my love; there is no flaw in you" (Song of Solomon 4:7).

» If you did, how might this affect how you get on with life and live fully to make God famous?

15

Love Scene

Love scene: An intimate scene between lovers, especially in a story or play. —*Oxford Dictionary*

> When I found him whom my soul loves.
> I held him, and would not let him go.

—SONG OF SOLOMON 3:4

Love scene. We've all seen them. I feel pretty awkward when I watch them, don't you? But we keep watching. We are drawn to them for many reasons, but one of which is the perfection of it all. You see two people in an ideal relationship maybe, with superb bodies and no problems. And even if they disagree, they make up beautifully—sometimes in a love scene. And we watch, wondering what that temporary realism must be like and maybe longing for it to be our own. Oh, the magic of Hollywood.

But it ain't reality. For anyone. Sometimes I watch relationships on screen, married or not, and I think, *they make it look so easy.* But then I remember there's so much more to marriage than a screenwriter's dreams of perfection and the two hours of bliss we see in the movies. There's baggage we bring into marriages—hang-ups and pain—all of which can hurt a marriage. But God can also use the marriage partners as helpers to move beyond the past so that the two together can be a force for His glory.

* The Engagement Photo *

I'm currently celebrating 15 years of marriage with my husband. I'm sitting in our bedroom staring at our engagement photo, which looks very posed and forced—like I would ever sit on my hip in the dewy grass with my legs perfectly placed beside me and my head cocked to one side. And like Markus would ever kneel on one knee behind me, also cocking his head at the same angle as mine. And like all of this would take place camera left of a perfect fountain of water spewing from the middle of a clear lake in the Fort Worth Botanic Gardens.

After laughing at the picture's lack of spontaneity, I remember how I felt while I sat there. I was in love with Markus on a high, ignorant level. Like big, fat crush, hormone-pumping love. He could do no wrong, and even if he did, I let it slide off of me like a pat of butter on warm toast. And yet now the love I feel for him and from him is nothing like I could have ever imagined sitting there in the damp grass that day. We've been through high highs and even lower lows. I share everything with him, and he with me. He makes me better—he doesn't say things to side with me when he senses I have my index finger selfishly pointed toward my chest. Instead he responds to encourage and challenge me, to steer me back toward looking like Jesus.

I can easily say I would be many years behind in my relationship with God if it weren't for Markus. This is what comes after years of being together and understanding that our job in marriage is to build the other up, emotionally and spiritually, and be moldable enough to allow this to happen. That marriage is supposed to make me look more like Christ and reflect the relationship of Christ and His Church, not be lived like an imaginary love scene. After 15 years, I'm understanding this now. Though I spent the early years of our marriage criticizing Markus when he failed to make me feel like Cinderella. And I'll be honest. I'm tempted every day to be overcritical of him.

* What Marriage Does *

If you had asked me, prewedding, if I considered myself selfless, I would've proudly said *yes*. But a little while as Mrs. Lloyd brought out my true colors because marriage unveiled the true me.

Engaged at 23, I had no idea how becoming a wife would change me, challenge me, break me, shape me, and force me to die to myself if I wanted our marriage to last.

I spent years refusing to see the log in my own eye while pointing out the splinter in his. I tried to get Markus to think and act like me and have the same priorities. And because I was so busy trying to convince him to be minime, I didn't appreciate how God had uniquely made him. I only saw Markus as wrong and needing to change. I spent years living for my happiness while hoping in the meantime Markus was happy too. But what I've learned so far in 15 short years of marriage is that when I'm living selflessly toward my husband and doing what I know I need to do to be an example of Jesus to him, I care more about Markus's happiness than I do my own.

And to get there and *stay* there each day, I have to die to "me."

* The Marriage Ender *

Because of its difficulty—and its beauty—marriage is supposed to set me apart for the glory of God and bring me closer to Christ so that I look more like Him and make Him famous—to my husband and the world around me.

Maybe, if you examine your marriage, you'll see, as I did, selfishness thick in the center of it, both your selfishness and your husband's. This focus on self comes straight from the inventor of it—Satan.

As soon as a couple gets married, Satan is working to destroy this covenant contract between two people and God. It's the strongest commitment two people can make on earth. So if Satan can rip up that contract, he's won. And he won't give up until the marriage is destroyed. He will continue to work to separate two married people until they die. Think of it like being in a war with no relief until death on the battlefield. Marriage is serious business—to God and to Satan. It's a big deal to God because marriage is a picture of God's relationship to us and has the potential to make Him famous. And it's a big deal to Satan for the exact same reasons.

Satan is the master of selfishness. It was his desire to be like God, his focus on himself, that got him kicked out of the presence of God. "Your heart was proud because of your beauty; you corrupted your wisdom for the sake of your splendor. I cast you to the ground" (Ezekiel 28:17).

Anytime we see Satan at work in Scripture, he's tempting people to think of themselves. He works to exploit the sin nature that is within us. And he will work to get us to think of ourselves, capitalizing on our sinful desires, in order to end our marriages and our godly relationships. Right before Jesus launched into His ministry, Satan used the "elevation of self" to tempt Jesus. While Satan didn't know all that Jesus would do with His ministry, he knew Jesus was a threat. And Satan knows our marriages are a threat to him too.

Satan tempted Jesus three times, and each time, he tried to entice Jesus to think about Himself.

Jesus fasted in the wilderness for 40 days before Satan showed up to tempt Him. So Satan offered to satisfy Jesus' deep hunger when he said, "If you are the Son of God, command these stones to become loaves of bread" (Matthew 4:3).

Then Satan tempted Jesus to put Himself above the authority of God—the exact thing he did to Adam and Eve in the garden. And Satan used Scripture to justify why Jesus should.

Then the devil took him to the holy city and set him on the pinnacle of the temple and said to him, "If you are the Son of God, throw yourself down, for it is written, 'He will command his angels concerning you,' and 'On their hands they will bear you up, lest you strike your foot against a stone.'"

—vv. 5-6

And finally, Satan offered Jesus more wealth than anyone had on earth, if only Jesus would call Satan lord.

Again, the devil took him to a very high mountain and showed him all the kingdoms of the world and their glory. And he said to him, "All these I will give you, if you will fall down and worship me."

—vv. 8-9

So how did Jesus fight back? With the Word of truth.

To the temptation for food, He said, "It is written, 'Man shall not live by bread alone, but by every word that comes from the mouth of God'" (v. 4).

To the temptation to put Himself above the authority of God, He said, "Again it is written, 'You shall not put the Lord your God to the test'" (v. 7).

To the temptation for wealth, Jesus replied, "Be gone, Satan! For it is written, 'You shall worship the Lord your God and Him only shall you serve'" (v. 10).

So how do we fight the war on our marriages so that God wins? Anytime we feel "me" rising to the surface, we must push ourselves back down with the truth of Scripture. It is our weapon. "In all circumstances take up . . . the sword of the Spirit, which is the word of God" (Ephesians 6:16–17). We must spend time with the Word of God to know the difference between what our flesh is saying and what God is saying. Otherwise, I'll choose me every time.

We also benefit from hanging around other couples who have strong marriages and friends who are willing to speak truth to us, not just what we want to hear. And we must recognize who we are really fighting within our marriage.

{ *For our struggle is not against flesh and blood, but against the rulers, against the authorities, against the powers of this dark world and against the spiritual forces of evil in the heavenly realms.* }

—EPHESIANS 6:12 NIV

And in addition to the enemy, our sin nature rears its ugly head and drags us into the deep abyss of "me-ness." I need Jesus to remind me on a constant basis that I am His earthly ambassador to my husband to help him be the best man he can be. If I want to live up to this awesome job, I need to be in constant communication with God so I hear His voice above the voice of the enemy and the voice of my own flesh.

* Change Me, Not Him *

Years into marriage, I was folding laundry on the couch and was mad at Markus because he had done something that again proved how opposite we were. But I was tired of being frustrated with Markus. And the Lord told me it was time to start responding differently to him—to his face and privately in my heart.

I told the Lord I desperately wanted to become selfless toward my husband. I wanted to recognize it was Satan and my flesh who were my enemies when Markus and I didn't get along. Markus wasn't my enemy. I wanted to cheer Markus on, be his biggest fan, and be as selfless as I could, but I needed God's help. I needed Him to convict me when I became selfish. I knew this would be hard, but I was ready to change.

I asked God to give me eyes to see Markus as God did. To appreciate how God had wired him. When I was tempted to choose me, I asked God to remind me to choose Him. To help me assume the best of Markus rather than the worst. And to reveal His heart for my husband to me and melt my heart into His.

And slowly—oh, so slowly—it happened. I realized, as God changed me, I saw Markus differently. I finally appreciated Markus and all the ways he was different from me rather than praying God would change him. God showed me that marriage really is not about me or the joy I get from it but about making me look more like Jesus.

I noticed I was no longer jealous of his success but, rather, excited for his opportunities. I looked for ways to serve him, instead of waiting for opportunities to stare me down. When my "self" rose to the surface, I pushed back the lies with Scripture I'd memorized and the prompting of the Holy Spirit.

This took effort and time. But I saw myself transform into a more holy Lisa rather than a trying-to-be-happy Lisa. And surprisingly, I was happier dying to myself and putting my husband ahead of me than living the way I had up until then. And I reflected the image of God. This is something I continue to work at and will continue to strive toward for the rest of my life. But I really want to do well.

You and I are not perfect and won't always care more for our spouse's happiness than our own. And our husbands won't always care more for our happiness than theirs. So we must not expect them to make us entirely happy. God must fill our happiness tank. And out of that filling we can selflessly make God famous to our spouse.

Imagine a marriage where spouses fight for the happiness of and the opportunity to serve the other? Tension in marriage would dissolve because people wouldn't focus on themselves but on the glory of God through them.

If both spouses truly worked hard to serve and love the other, imagine how that marriage would make God famous.

This is possible. Easy? Nope. But possible? Yes. And worth it. For our happiness, holiness, and the glory of God.

Questions to Consider:

» If you are married, in what specific ways do you find your "self" rising up against your husband?

» Do you believe the best about him? If not, why not? If so, how?

» What is one thing you can do today to make God famous to your husband? How will you do it?

» What is another thing you can change about yourself long-term to make God famous to your husband? How will you do it?

16

The Antagonist

{ *O Lord, how long shall the wicked, how long shall the wicked exult? They pour out their arrogant words; all the evildoers boast. They crush your people, O Lord, and afflict your heritage. They kill the widow and the sojourner, and murder the fatherless; and they say, "The Lord does not see; the God of Jacob does not perceive."* }

—PSALM 94:3–7

The antagonist is always the character the audience most dislikes—Joker, Lex Luthor, Cinderella's stepmother, and the Wicked Witch of the West. We always feel relief when they are ruined and get what they had coming to them. The antagonists are important because they often create the tension needed for a successful show.

Every year as a little girl, my family would vacation in the quaint mountain town of Red River, New Mexico. And every year, we would see a melodrama—an overly dramatic play with exaggerated characters and events. This family-friendly spectacle was set up to be an audience participation show for sure. When the ingénue (the innocent and unpolished heroine that every little girl wants to be when she grows up. Think Princess Buttercup from *The Princess Bride* or Anne Shirley from *Anne of Green Gables*) came onstage, the audience was invited to *oooooh* and *ahhhhh* dramatically. When the hero came on, the audience clapped and cheered. But when the villain appeared, everyone *booed* and threw their popcorn at him. The piano player sitting at the old upright piano in the audience played dramatic music to accompany the entrance of each character. The villain always turned the ingénue into a "damsel in distress," sometimes tying her to the "railroad tracks," and the hero had to save her. After a tussle here and a melodramatic fight there, the hero defeated the villain and took him to jail, and the audience cheered and whistled in victory.

* Beyond the Melodrama *

Audience members loved this show because it's exactly what they wanted to happen in everyday life. For a moment we could escape the reality of the world beyond the theater doors and know that justice was served. The antagonist was beaten by the hero protagonist, and everyone was safe. The audience was riveted, all while smelling freshly popped popcorn in the air and feeling the stickiness of dried soda on the floor under our feet.

But once we walked out of the theater doors, it was back to the reality that true injustice and terror lurked in pockets all over the world.

We see it on the nightly television news and on our news tickers across our smartphones. Injustice makes us ball our fists in anger because injustice is always against the innocent. My stomach churns when I think about it—like lava inside a volcano about to erupt. And injustice especially against women and children makes me want to throw something across the room.

* Nicaragua *

I served for a week at a safe house in Nicaragua a few years ago. This safe house was for women and their children escaping human trafficking and prostitution. So you can imagine, I spent a lot of my time there with my fists balled.

In Nicaragua, prostitution is illegal for those under the age of 14 but for those 14 and up? Well, they are fair game. Every morning we drove past brothels on our way to see the families who miraculously escaped such a life. We heard about the sex shops open 24/7 at the back of the shopping markets. At the safe house, we spoke with women who are now free from the terror of their pimps. But arriving at freedom wasn't easy. The women and their children trapped in this life are told from a young age that they are worthless, will never amount to anything, and are useful to men for only one thing—and they might as well get used to it. And parents, who should make their children feel safe, don't. When children are raped—which happened to so many of the women we spoke with when they were little girls—they are seen as "damaged goods," and many parents sell them into sex slavery. For the lucky few whose parents send them to the doctor after victimization, these girls often find themselves abused by the very doctor they thought would help.

It's sick.

But perhaps the most disturbing story I heard was from a woman named Daphne. Daphne's pimp slashed her face and cut off her arm when she told him she wanted to leave him. Somehow she eventually escaped. Daphne sat across from me as we gave the women at the safe house pedicures one afternoon. When I took her leg in my hands, I felt the lower half of her leg, thick with callouses—a result of being burned by her pimp. The only part of her legs free from burns was a small strip of flesh that ran the length of her calves. As we talked, she told me about her 12-year-old daughter who was sex trafficked by Daphne's former pimp and had a baby by him. Twelve. Years. Old.

Terror like this is known all over the world.

* Paris *

On the night of November 13, 2015, I stood in our kitchen with some friends from the neighborhood when one of them said, "Have you heard about the attacks in Paris?" I hadn't. As she unfolded the events of the day, my face was hot with anger and my helpless heart stood still. I turned on the TV to hear more about the tragic events I somehow missed earlier that day.

I learned there were seven coordinated terror attacks, killing at least 130 people. The attacks were carried out by suicide bombers and gunmen. The horror occurred outside a stadium during a soccer game, at three restaurants, at a bar, and at the Bataclan concert hall, where 89 of the victims were killed.

The next morning the terror group the Islamic State of Iraq and Syria (ISIS) claimed responsibility. My immediate and instinctive response? *I hope France and all her allies will bomb ISIS out of existence.* For hours I sat with this thought and imagined it taking place. I agreed with the verse, "When justice is done, it is a joy to the righteous but terror to evildoers" (Proverbs 21:15).

The Hebrew word for "justice," mishpat, occurs in its various forms more than 200 times in the Hebrew Old Testament.

* Angry and Helpless *

Let's not forget endless elementary, high school, movie theater, college, and church shootings. Or the corrupt Syrian government taking the innocent lives of those in their country. And maybe each time we hear about these ruthless individuals, you, like me, ask the questions, *Why do people think they can do this to another person? Who do they think they are? How lofty must one think themselves and how low must they think of others that committing these horrific crimes is permissible?*

* The Love and the Justice of God *

When there is such widespread terror and injustice, I feel angry and helpless. My heart echoes what the writer of this psalm said:

> { *O Lord, God of vengeance, O God of vengeance,*
> *shine forth! Rise up, O judge of the earth; repay to*
> *the proud what they deserve!* }

— PSALM 94:1–2

I believe the anger and rage within me is the Holy Spirit, who—while I can only *imagine* what happens to people terrorized by those set on evil—watches each awful moment.

God talks about how He *will* take His stand on the earth for those suffering, and He *will* carry out His vengeance. "Vengeance is mine, I will repay, says the Lord" (Romans 12:19). We can be confident the perpetrators will pay.

Yet, there is another side to God's character when it comes to injustice. And though it seems unfair to contemplate, I must meditate on it because it is God's heart—while He weeps for those who are left behind, He also weeps for those who are to blame. His heart is for justice but also for *redemption*. As He passionately pursued me, He passionately pursues the hearts of those who commit these crimes, those determined to take the lives of the innocent. God's deep desire is that those who bring death are brought to their knees before Him.

> God our Savior, who desires all people *to be saved and to come to the knowledge of the truth. For there is one God, and there is one mediator between God and men, the man Christ Jesus, who gave himself as a ransom for* all.
>
> −1 TIMOTHY 2:3−6 *(author's emphasis)*

Just like the criminal crucified on the cross next to Jesus, no one is beyond the love and forgiveness of Christ. We don't know what offense the crucified lawbreaker committed. Maybe he too victimized women and children. Or maybe he killed hundreds of innocent people. But in the presence of Jesus, he couldn't help but be broken by his sin and see his need for salvation. And Jesus couldn't help but accept him.

While hanging in agony, the criminal said to Him, "'Jesus, remember me when you come into your kingdom.' And [Jesus] said to him, 'Truly, I say to you, today you will be with me in paradise'" (Luke 23:42–43).

God aches for those bent on evil to recognize the terror of their ways, bow their knees to Him, and then tell anyone who will listen:

{ *Christ Jesus came into the world to save sinners, of whom I am the foremost. But I received mercy for this reason, that in me, as the foremost, Jesus Christ might display his perfect patience as an example to those who were to believe in him for eternal life.* }

—1 TIMOTHY 1:15-16

God wants to use the testimony of one to change one more and another and another. For His glory. In the life of Daphne's pimp, suicide bombers, the gunmen of ISIS, and countless others, He wants to be made famous. Now, imagine that for a moment.

In addition to praying for the justice God loves, I need to pray for those who pull a trigger and raise a machete.

As we have seen evidenced for thousands of years, God wants to change the hearts of those who are against Him for the spread of the gospel and the sake of His celebrity. I'm sure people would have never believed anything or anyone could change the hearts and minds of the criminal on the cross, or King Nebuchadnezzar (Daniel 4:34), or the woman at the well (John 4). Like these, I deeply believe God wants the redemption of those who seem the furthest from Him for the elevation of His name and His fame.

* I pray, I teach, and I fight. *

When my husband hears me get worked up and emotional about those who ruin or take the lives of the innocent, he almost always asks me, "So what are you going to do about it?" to which I now respond, "I pray, I teach, and I fight."

I *pray* for these criminals; as much as it pains me, I pray for their salvation. And in humility I recognize that in God's eyes, my sin is no different than theirs. We are all sinners who need the sanctification of a Savior. So I keep praying for them.

And I *teach* my boys how to treat and respect others, because God made them. All life is precious. We may not always agree with what people believe, but we love them and show them love regardless. Bullying is never allowed, and we use our tongues to build up not tear down.

I especially teach my boys to respect women for the amazing creatures they are. To cherish them and to see them as God sees them.

And using the gifts God's given me, I *fight* against the horrific crimes that ignite the desire for justice within me. It's my opinion that much of the sex trafficking happening in America is because children don't value their bodies, and they feel like they don't belong, which adds to their low self-esteem. So when someone who is secretly eyeing them for trafficking offers sex disguised as love and a place to find identity, the child is seduced and sucked in. I think a start to the solution is to teach young boys and girls that they are valued, loved, worth it, treasured, purchased, perfect, and they don't need to give themselves away to find their identity.

My friend Marquita and I created a proactive parent workshop, "Konfident Kids," designed to teach parents how to keep their kids safe from sex abuse. We equip parents of all backgrounds, nationalities, and religious beliefs with body safety rules to teach and empower their children to keep themselves safe but also show them that they are valuable and worthy. And because in more than 90 percent of cases, the child knows their abuser, we educate parents about how to screen caregivers and to recognize how a predator grooms children and parents to trust them. As a result, we hope to keep innocent kids innocent and predators at bay. But all the while, we pray for the salvation of perpetrators.

We all must pray, teach, and fight.

What injustice makes you ball your fists in anger? What churns your stomach? Then I ask you, as Markus asks me, "So what are you going to do about it?" You can volunteer with an organization already on the frontlines, you can raise awareness, or you can join a movement. We can all pray, teach, and fight.

So, while I can't raid a brothel—except in my imagination—I can ruin the enemy's plan of attack in my corner of the world. And while I await Christ's return, I can partner with Him in His fight for justice. But I won't turn a blind eye.

Can you imagine what might happen to the image of God around the world if even a few pimps and ISIS members bowed their knees, not to radical terrorism, but to a radical Jesus?

If only a few dedicated their lives, not to the hurting of innocent people, but to the life-giving salvation of Jesus Himself?

If a handful of the antagonists put down their weapons and picked up their crosses?

Imagine how people would stop, watch, and ask, "What could be so powerful to melt the heart of a murderer?"

I believe this is possible because this is what God desires. We *must* pray to that end.

May we ache for justice as God does. "For I the LORD love justice" (Isaiah 61:8). And may we pray for the salvation of those who have yet to accept it.

> The Lord is not slow to fulfill his promise as some count slowness, but is patient toward you, not wishing that any should perish, but that all should reach repentance.

—2 PETER 3:9 *(author's emphasis)*

And may we, and former pimps and terrorists, make God famous.

Questions to Consider:

» What injustice makes you ball your fists in anger?

» How did the statement about God's character, "While He weeps for those who are left behind, He also weeps for those who are to blame," make you feel?

» Can you think of someone who has refused the love and forgiveness of Jesus because of their rebellion against Him?

» Can you imagine what their life might be like if they bowed their knees to Jesus? Who might take notice in their sphere of influence? How might this make God famous to those people?

» How will you pray? Who will you teach? How will you fight?

17

Stage Mom

Stage mom: Pushy, obnoxious, crazy mothers who force their kids to act, model, or enter beauty contests, usually turning them into emotionally scared adults who hate their parents. —*Urban Dictionary*

> *Hear, O Israel: The LORD our God, the LORD is one.*
> *Love the LORD your God with all your heart and with all your soul and*
> *with all your strength. These commandments that I give you today*
> *are to be on your hearts. Impress them on your children. Talk about*
> *them when you sit at home and when you walk along the road,*
> *when you lie down and when you get up. Tie them as symbols on*
> *your hands and bind them on your foreheads. Write them on the*
> *doorframes of your houses and on your gates.*

—DEUTERONOMY 6:4–9 NIV

Nowadays, when I'm cast in a commercial, I'm almost always cast as a mom. And usually, I'm cast with kids. And of course, the mamas of these kids accompany them to the shoot. I've had some amazing conversations with these moms and almost always leave the shoot having made a new friend. Although I've never worked with a stereotypical "stage mom," I've heard stories. A casting director, Kelly, told me she is no longer on social media because the moms of the kids she auditioned would stalk her. They would message her with questions: *Did my kid have a good audition? Will he get a callback? When will we know if she books? Just checking in again . . . Kelly, Kelly? Did you get my message, hello?* Luckily for the kid, the obsessive stage mom didn't have an effect on the kid getting cast. Kelly told me, "It's not the kid's fault the mom is crazy."

Some "stage moms" live in the past. They were successful performers and need their kids to be the same. Others can be insecure and need to know their kid is the best. The way they gain security is to constantly put their kids in competitive environments that affirm the mom and their child.

But there is one trait that all stereotypical stage moms share: they see the end, and they go after it. They do all they can today to get their kid to the finish line.

Sometimes I'll take my kids to an audition. Since I know what it takes to have a successful audition, it's hard not to become a nagging stage mom. "Remember to smile." "But don't oversmile." "Speak up." "Act like you love the product you're auditioning with." "Did you brush your teeth?" "Use your manners." "Keep your hands out of your pockets." "Let's rehearse that again." These are just a few of the lines I've heard exit my mouth.

As moms, whether our kid is an actor, a ball player, a musician, or destined for Harvard, we see the end and know what it takes to get there, or at least we think we do, so it's tempting to push and sometimes overpush our kids to the finish line.

But do we push with even greater fervor to the finish line of helping our kids become Christ followers who make a difference in those environments? Do we want success or fame for them, or is the vision of success we cast that of making God famous?

And like Reggie Joiner, author of the book *Think Orange,* says if we want our kids to love God with everything in them and live it out, we must imagine the end. *Who* do I want my kids to become?

And then we reverse engineer and parent today with that end in mind. The best way to do this in my opinion is to embrace teachable moments. I once had a larger than life teachable moment on a visit to the mall with my oldest son, Deuce.

* Look Away from the Naked Woman! *

We came upon a lingerie store with a gargantuan poster of a busty bra model.

I tried to distract him by pointing out the LEGO store right around the corner. But he ran over to the poster and stood underneath the "angelic" woman. His eyes told me "heaven" was right here.

I watched as chuckling adults passed him by. They laughed and said to each other how "cute" this was. But it was far from cute to me. I was embarrassed, and all I wanted to do was pick him up, ignore what was happening, and find a cookie counter to distract him. But what I had in front of me, in addition to a boy drooling over beauty, was a teachable moment. Despite my desire to run, I decided to engage. I walked over, passing the snickering mall-goers, and stood by my son. "She's beautiful isn't she, buddy?"

"Yeah, Mom. *Ohhh yeah.*" His eyes stayed glued on the image.

Good grief. I knelt next to him and continued.

"As you grow, there are going to be many women you'll see who will model like this. They will be everywhere—on TV, on billboards, and in the mall. As a man, you will be drawn to want to look at them. But you have the opportunity to not only protect your mind from the forever stamp of this image, but you also have the chance to show her respect when you turn your head or close your eyes. And when you do this, you are telling her you don't have to look at her like that to see her beauty. Because women are beautiful because God made them, not because they show their skin."

It's times like these when God reminds us that our jobs, whether parents or guardians or grandparents, is to help shape and mold our kids' character. Because kids with character can change the world— or at least their little corner of it. We can empower them to impact their communities, neighborhoods, workplaces, and families—no matter their age or ours. All for the glory of God.

A couple days later, we were at home watching TV when a commercial came on advertising an outdoor water toy. A little girl, who couldn't have been more than six years old, was wearing a bikini and splashing in the water. Deuce immediately put his hands over his eyes, almost at attention. When he could hear that the commercial was over, he dropped his hands, looked at me with his toothless grin, and gave me two thumbs up.

I can't protect my kids from every negative influence, person, or image, but I can embrace teachable moments to help my kids become the men I've envisioned them becoming. Men who love God with everything in them. Who choose Jesus at every turn. Who are willing to be made fun of, who are willing to be persecuted, who are willing to risk it all to live for the fame of God's name.

It's not the church's responsibility to help my kids become this. It's *my* responsibility, the parent. God tells us so.

In Deuteronomy 6, Moses commands parents, guardians, and all of the believing community to teach our kids to love God with everything in them. But his first command was to the adults.

> Hear, O Israel: The LORD our God, the LORD is one. Love the LORD your God with all your heart and with all your soul and with all your strength. *These commandments that I give you today are to be on your hearts.*

—DEUTERONOMY 6:4–6 NIV *(author's emphasis)*

Moses knew the Israelites were headed to the Promised Land, where they would encounter enemies of God. The Israelites were God's people, chosen to reflect His image to the entire world, so they couldn't follow what the world followed and love what the world loved—possessions, money, sex, the elevation of self, just to name a few of the world's vices. So God had to be their number one, or they would forget Him and become like everyone else.

Do we deeply love God with all our heart, soul, and strength? Do we value what He does? As broken people, we won't always. And we will often choose ourselves over God. But in our heart of hearts, are our intentions and endeavors reflective of loving God more than anything else? This, I believe, is what loving God with all our heart, soul, and strength looks like.

God continues—

{ *These commandments that I give you today are to be on your* }
hearts. Impress them on your children.

—DEUTERONOMY 6:6–7 NIV

The purpose of parenting is not my happiness. It's not my comfort. It's not passing along traditions that I grew up with or making sure my kid is happy. If we want a kid who's going to choose God at every turn, these temporary things can't be our focus.

The purpose of parenting, and therefore my job as a mom, is to partner with God to shape the spiritual trajectory of my kids' lives so that they leave my home bent on making God famous.

So I imagine what I want my kids to look like, not academically or athletically but spiritually, when they leave my home, understanding that life really is all about God. And I imagine the end, reverse engineer, and parent today with that end in mind.

But how do we parent our kids to live this way? God gives us a great idea.

{ *Talk about them [the commandments] when you sit at home* }
and when you walk along the road, when you lie down and
when you get up. Tie them as symbols on your hands and
bind them on your foreheads. Write them on the doorframes
of your houses and on your gates.

—DEUTERONOMY 6:7–9 NIV

We teach our kids as we are going—while watching TV, in the car, at the dinner table, at bedtime, via text message or social media. Basically wherever we are, we embrace the teachable moments we find ourselves in and lead there.

* We Parent What We Believe *

My counselor once told me in a session, we "parent what we believe." In other words, whatever we value is exactly what we will pass on to our children. If we value environmental responsibility, a love for the poor, not having debt, or showing respect to a lingerie store model by turning our heads when we see them, we will pass our values onto our kids. Our kids will pick up on it because *we* see it as significant.

So I asked myself, "How am I parenting what I believe?"

I realized there were some not-so-great things I believe, and I've passed these on to my children. Like thinking my way is the *only* way to do something. It is, of course, but may not be the best thing to teach my kids.

But I also realized I'm passing great beliefs on to my kids. I know I'm not the best parent. I know I'm a young parent. And I know I still have a long way to go and a lot to learn. But because Markus and I parent what we believe, we see our kids working to love God and love others better. We work to embrace God's command to love Him whole-heartedly and pass on what He values to our kids so they will live the same. We do our best to take advantage of the teachable moments we find ourselves in. And God willing, they will grow into kids who make God famous. Here are some of the values we pass on to our kids.

LLOYDS DON'T LIE.

{ *Do not lie to one another, seeing that you have put off the old self with its practices.* }

—COLOSSIANS 3:9

As a child, I would lie to my parents to avoid getting into trouble. I knew that if I lied, I had a one in two chance of getting away with what I'd done. Most kids think like this. *Why would I tell mom the truth if lying might save me from punishment?* When we lie, we don't align ourselves with God's ways, and it becomes easier and easier for us to lie once we start down that road. One little lie leads to another and another, and before we know it, we are further from God than we ever imagined we'd be when we lied in the first place. Markus and I tell our boys, "Lloyds don't lie." We don't lie to our kids to make them feel better or make a situation easier, and they aren't allowed to lie either. If they are in the wrong but tell us the truth, they don't get into trouble. And even if they made a bad choice, like hitting their brother, but tell us they did so, we praise them for telling the truth and correct the behavior, but they don't have consequences. Our kids admit wrong and tell the truth almost every time. This has made the traditions of Santa, the Easter bunny, and the tooth fairy difficult. So we don't. Tough? Yep. But we believe it's worth it.

THE BIBLE IS THE BEST BOOK ON THE PLANET. IT'S OUR ANSWER SOURCE.

{ *Blessed is the one . . . whose delight is in the law of the* Lord, *and who meditates on his law day and night.* }

—PSALM 1:1–2 NIV

The Bible gives us clarity when our world is spinning in confusion. When our kids go through a tough situation, we steer them to Scripture to find their answer. The Word is where we can literally *see* God speaking to us, guiding, encouraging, and loving us.

We encourage our boys to read their Bibles before they come downstairs in the morning. Do they do this faithfully every morning? Nope, not always. But we're working on it. We want them to see the value of God's Word, to read it, and apply it. After they've read in the morning, or when we pick them up from class at church on Sundays, I ask them, "Retell me the story." "What is something cool you learned about God?" "How can you apply this story to your life?" Often I have to help them answer these—and often among shouts from the back of the van, "What's for lunch?" But I embrace these teachable moments so my kids know that the Bible is more than just a book about good overcoming evil with stories of war and death and heroes and villains. Although, my boys do love this about the Bible. The Bible can transform our lives if we allow it to.

{ *For the word of God is alive and active. Sharper than any double-edged sword, it penetrates even to dividing soul and spirit, joints and marrow; it judges the thoughts and attitudes of the heart.* }

—HEBREWS 4:12 NIV

WE PRAY FOR OTHERS.

{ *Praying at all times in the Spirit, with all prayer and supplication. To that end, keep alert with all perseverance, making supplication for all the saints.* }

—EPHESIANS 6:18

Prayer for others puts our focus on someone other than ourselves. Hard to do at any age, isn't it? I ask my kids to pray for me. "And [pray] also for me, that words may be given to me in opening my mouth boldly to proclaim the mystery of the gospel" (Ephesians 6:19). This shows them I believe God will listen to *their* prayers for me. I was nervous for a recent speaking engagement and asked our youngest son, Solomon, to pray for me. When I returned from the talk, Solomon said, "I asked God to help you not be scared and for you to remember God is with you. Just like I remember when I'm scared of the dark." Awesome.

It's easy for our kids to get in the habit of praying a "rote prayer" and saying the same thing in the same order every night. We don't want our kids to talk to God like a robot. Instead we want them to realize they can intercede for others, ask God for big things, and watch as He answers them. To break out of the robot routine, we encourage our kids to ask God to help or meet the needs of someone they know. Maybe a kid in their class who needs help or who is having a hard time with self-control *(which actually might have been one of our kids)*. And before they finish praying to also ask God for something they need or want to see happen in their lives, even if it was something silly, like extra video game time. It's been fun to ask our kids about how God has answered their prayers and watch them beam as they tell us. And I worship as I see how He's making Himself famous to them.

We remind them that praying can happen all day long. They can pray silently to themselves at school before they take a test, as they are walking to lunch, or if they see a kid hurt on the playground. God loves to answer their prayers. Even if the answer is no, God is always listening and wants to hear from them.

OBEY QUICKLY.

{ *I hasten and do not delay to keep your commandments.* }

—PSALM 119:60

Not only does God want us to obey Him but to obey Him quickly. Many of us grew up in a house where if we didn't do what our parents instructed, they counted to three before they punished us. This communicated to us that we could continue to disobey until our parents got to two and three quarters, right? When we teach our kids to obey us quickly, we also teach them to obey God quickly.

CHOOSE FRIENDS THAT MAKE YOU BETTER, AND HAVE THE COURAGE TO RELEASE FRIENDS THAT DO NOT.

{ *One who is righteous is a guide to his neighbor, but the way of the wicked leads them astray.* }

—PROVERBS 12:26

{ *Whoever walks with the wise becomes wise, but the companion of fools will suffer harm.* }

—PROVERBS 13:20

One of my kiddos loves the "spotlight." He enjoys being the center of attention and will sometimes choose to receive a laugh or be liked rather than to do the right thing. This often results in him passing up the opportunity to make a good choice. As a result, we teach our kids there are times we need to walk away from bad influences so we are not dragged down into mimicking their behavior. This is the harder, unpopular choice, but it can be done. And when done, it glorifies God.

But there are other times when we cannot get away from negative influences—when we are at school or on the soccer team. So what do we do then? We sat on our "spotlight" son's bed one night, and Markus explained a line he read in Martin Luther King Jr.'s, *Letter from Birmingham Jail*. King talked about how we should be a thermostat instead of a thermometer in our world. A thermometer becomes the temperature of what's around it while a thermostat adjusts the temperature. Markus challenged our son to be a thermostat every day. And now he sends our boys off to school saying, "Go be a thermostat, son, go be a thermostat."

My kids may change their behaviors for a while, to please me, but at some point, their decisions have to be something they *want* to do. I pray they choose to leave the comfort of bad influences because they want God more than they want the convenience of their flesh. And when they can't leave, I pray they choose to be a thermostat.

CONFESS AND ASK FORGIVENESS.

> *If we confess our sins, he is faithful and just to forgive us our sins and cleanse us from all unrighteousness.*
>
> —1 JOHN 1:9

In her book, *The Power of a Praying Parent*, Stormie Omartian offers up a prayer for parents to pray for their kids. "[That if our kid sins], may she (he) be so miserable that confession and its consequences will seem like a relief." I pray this now for my kids. I also realize I must lead by example and ask for my kids' forgiveness when I screw up. This teaches them I am not perfect and shows them how to admit when they are wrong. Years ago, I listened to a podcast that featured Rob Rienow, author of *Visionary Parenting*. He suggested that the way to ask forgiveness is like this: "I did 'X,' I was wrong, please forgive me." Confession and repentance are a healing balm for any relationship.

STAND IN AWE OF GOD.

Yours, O LORD, is the greatness and the power and the glory and the victory and the majesty, for all that is in the heavens and in the earth is yours. Yours is the kingdom, O LORD, and you are exalted as head above all.

−1 CHRONICLES 29:11

I sometimes stand in awe of God. It can come from a majestic thunderstorm or a hymm streaming on my device as I clean the kitchen. I try to point these ties out to my kids. I may call them over to listen or observe what I see and feel about God. Often they just politely listen, but they don't feel what I do, at least not at the same level. But that's OK because at least they are watching Mommy worship. They are watching me stand in awe of God. And maybe one day, they too will mirror me. As they remember those times by the stormy window or in the car or at home hearing worship music play, they will be drawn in to worship their Creator who deserves all our worship.

VALUE PURITY, AND FLEE THE TEMPTATION OF PORN AND SEX.

So flee youthful passions and pursue righteousness, faith, love, and peace, along with those who call on the Lord from a pure heart.

−2 TIMOTHY 2:22

God created man and woman to be together in marriage, and any sexual relationship outside of that, though difficult for hormone-racing kids to resist, is not how God planned and will therefore be a great disappointment. The blessing of God comes when a man and woman are married and can enjoy each other fully as God intended.

Pornography is dangerous. It's not reflective of reality, and it pushes boys to expect behaviors of girls that are not realistic. In my opinion, it is a conduit to the sex industry and human trafficking, which demeans women and men.

And I believe the fight for our kids' hearts when it comes to porn and sex is won with open communication and open hearts. We must share with our kids our own struggles and mistakes in this area. This is an absolute must. Fear tactics and punishment for poor sexual behavior will push our kids so far away from us we will never have their trust.

Every time, every single time, I speak to Christian teens about my story of premarital sex and abortion, they come up to me and thank me for being real. They talk about how what I shared made them feel not so alone and how they wished they could hear other believers talk about this too, especially their parents. Their parents, they say, have told them what not to do and how God disapproves. When I ask, "Have your parents ever shared with you their own mistakes as a teen?" They quickly say, "Oh, my gosh, no way! They would never do that!" So these teens have concluded that their parents don't "get" them and will be infuriated if they tell them their boyfriend is pushing them to have sex or if they've had sex with their girlfriend, but they want to stop or don't know how.

We've communicated repetitive, "don'ts" and "nevers" to our kids. This message is understandable, and—don't get me wrong—we want our kids to "flee youthful passions," but we also don't want them living secret lives, afraid and running to their peers for support, which is what they are doing. It's what I did, and maybe you too. We must communicate to our kids that there's nothing they could do to escape Mom and Dad's love for them. Or the love of Jesus.

> { *For I am sure that neither death nor life, nor angels nor rulers,*
> *nor things present nor things to come, nor powers, nor height*
> *nor depth, nor anything else in all creation, will be able to*
> *separate us from the love of God in Christ Jesus our Lord.* }
>
> —ROMANS 8:38–39

We need to tell them our own stories so they feel safe coming to us. Just like we've received the forgiveness and love of Jesus, we extend that to them too. Their choices will never affect how much we love them. It's easy to assume kids know this, but they need to be reminded again and again. Just like Jesus, our love knows no conditions.

We want to help them, not scare them into obedience.

"MAKE SURE YOU DATE SOMEONE YOU COULD MARRY BECAUSE ONE DAY YOU WILL MARRY SOMEONE YOU DATED."

Therefore a man shall leave his father and his mother and hold fast to his wife, and they shall become one flesh.

— GENESIS 2:24

My mom said this to me over and over when I was a teenager. At the time, I wanted to tell her where she could stick her annoying advice. But once I got to college, I learned she was brilliant. Outside of a relationship with God, who our children marry is the most important decision they will ever make. A spouse will bring us closer to or further away from God. And who we marry can set the route for the rest of our lives. I'm already praying for my kids' spouses and for my boys to set high standards for a dating and marriage partner and refuse to lower them.

I'm casting the vision for them to run hard after Jesus. Then one day, they look over to their right or left and see a gal also running hard after Jesus, and they say, "Let's do this life together and become a force for the kingdom." I will encourage them to set their standards high and never lower them. But also remember that someone running hard after Jesus will be attracted to someone else running hard too, not someone they have to pull along. They should strive to become the kind of person they want to marry.

GOD HAS BIG PLANS FOR YOU.
POINT EVERYTHING YOU DO BACK TO HIM.

Everyone who is called by my name, whom I created for my glory, whom I formed and made.

— ISAIAH 43:7

No matter what God has you doing or where He has you doing it—baseball, soccer, piano, playing with friends, hanging out at home, or working at school—He put you on this planet to make His name great. To make Him famous. Whatever you do and say should be for His glory:

> *Whoever speaks, as one who speaks oracles of God; whoever serves, as one who serves by the strength that God supplies—in order that in everything God may be glorified through Jesus Christ. To him belong glory and dominion forever and ever. Amen.*

> —1 PETER 4:11

Life isn't about you or your comfort. Life is all about Him.

Throughout each teachable moment, I try to share how I too struggled in some way with what my kids are going through. I believe our stories of vulnerability will show our kids we are real, approachable, flawed, and that they can learn from our mistakes rather than their own.

Now, it would be ignorant of me to suggest, "Imagine the end, parent with the end in mind, embrace teachable moments, and your kids will end up making great choices." There's no guarantee this will happen. They will make decisions that don't line up with what we value. But since our kids borrow their self-esteem from us until they are old enough to develop their own, again, they must know our love has no restrictions.

* Spring Breakers *

When Deuce was younger, he asked to stream a movie on my tablet, and I said yes. That night he came downstairs into the living room and said he couldn't sleep. He told Markus and me his stomach was tight, and he had to tell us something but was nervous to do so. I could sense he had something to confess. Immediately, I thanked God for answering my prayer about him being miserable until he brought his sin into the light. We reminded him that if he confessed to us, he wouldn't get into trouble. Quite the opposite. He could count on us to give him a big hug and commend his bravery for telling us. After a little more encouragement, he went on to tell us that after he had permission to watch the first show, he selected a second movie, *Spring Breakers*.

Oh, for the love.

He said he knew he shouldn't watch it, but he was curious and only watched two minutes of it. Sure enough when I went to look at my device, *Spring Breakers* was paused at 2:03, but during that time he said he saw a girl who was in a bikini and another girl who took her bikini top off. He was only five years old! And I was ready to burn Hollywood down.

It was remarkable to watch the Holy Spirit work within little Deuce. He felt so awful about what he saw, and I told him to always pay attention to that voice telling him to make a good choice because that is the Holy Spirit convicting him so that he would confess and walk away from his sin. "Anyone who hides their sins doesn't succeed. But anyone who admits their sins and gives them up finds mercy" (Proverbs 28:13 NIrV). We praised him for telling us and identified with his feelings saying, "It must have been very hard to tell us, buddy. But we are so proud of you." We went on to talk about what he can do the next time he wants to watch a movie like this—but, this won't be necessary because I will have taken out all of Hollywood with my swinging handbag.

Markus vulnerably identified with Deuce and talked about the difficult struggle guys have in this area—Daddy, too. He told Deuce that they would need to help and pray for each other. He encouraged Deuce by telling him his desires were good and that one day, he will get to look at his wife the same way he wants to look at that girl in the movie. God put those desires within him but for a special time and woman. We hugged and prayed and Deuce went back to bed with much more peace than when he came downstairs. Satan, you lost that one.

* Brave Parenting *

Parenting with the end in mind is brave parenting. It's countercultural. It's others-focused. It's God-focused. And it's hard. No doubt, parenting with the end in mind and sticking with it will mean you will stand alone most days. Your kids will stand alone. But they will make a statement as they refuse their flesh to love God with everything in them and make Him famous.

This may be a completely new parenting approach for you because maybe your parents never raised you this way. Maybe your parents left the teaching of God and the rearing of your spiritual soul to Sunday School teachers. Maybe your parents didn't know God or never heard Deuteronomy 6.

Maybe you feel alone in the fight for the spiritual hearts of your kids because you're a single parent or at least feel that way because your husband couldn't be less involved. Or you've believed the lie that since you've not parented this way thus far, and your kids are teenagers, what's the use?

Maybe you're an empty nester, and you feel "parenting with the end in mind" is a lost cause because your kids are grown and living their own lives.

It's never too late.

No matter your current situation, you can cast a vision of God's fame to your kids, encourage them in the choices they are making, embrace teachable moments, talk about God on a regular basis, share what God is teaching you, and pray for your kids on the phone, via text, and even social media. However you communicate to your kids, you can "impress" the principles of God to them (Deuteronomy 6:7 NIV). You will never stop being a parent. So you will never lose the opportunity to parent with the end in mind.

Today you can decide to break the chain that keeps your parenting bound to the past and "the way it's always been." Today you can take the responsibility and the charge from God to love Him with everything in you and pass that along to your kids, no matter their age or your situation. Imagine what embracing this might look like for generations after you. Talk about leaving a legacy.

There is no other person in our child's life with the potential to have such a great impact, to shape and mold their character, and to teach them that life's all about God more than a parent. As stereotypical "stage moms" imagine the end and do all they can today to get their kids to the finish line of fame, let's redeem this idea in our context. Let's become "spiritual stage moms" as we imagine the end of our kids' time in our homes, reverse engineer, and parent today with that end in mind. And as a result of our brave parenting, may our kids, grandkids, and generations after them live to make God famous.

Questions to Consider:

» Are there areas in your parenting where you, like me, are tempted to become a "stage mom"? Football, academics, music?

» How would you like your child(ren) to look spiritually when they leave your home? What characteristics would they exude? What would they value?

» If they have already left your home, how would you like to see them impact their world?

» In what ways can you change, or continue, what you are doing to parent with this end in mind?

» How can you show your child unconditional love?

» What mistakes from your past could you share with your child that might help them not make the choices you did? How do you think your vulnerability will make you more approachable to them?

» What obstacles do you anticipate as you parent with the end in mind?

18

Actors, the Opposite of People

There we were—demented children mincing about in clothes that no one ever wore, speaking as no man ever spoke, swearing love in wigs and rhymed couplets, killing each other with wooden swords, hollow protestations of faith hurled after empty promises of vengeance—and every gesture, every pose, vanishing into the thin unpopulated air. We ransomed our dignity to the clouds, and the uncomprehending birds listened. Don't you see?! We're actors—we're the opposite of people!

—from Tom Stoppard's, *Rosencrantz and Guildenstern are Dead*

Still he seeks the fellowship of his people and sends them both sorrows and joys in order to detach their love from other things and attach it to Himself.

—J. I. Packer

Has the LORD as great delight in burnt offerings and sacrifices, as in obeying the voice of the LORD? Behold, to obey is better than sacrifice, and to listen than the fat of rams.

—1 SAMUEL 15:22

Actors make a lot of sacrifices for their craft—sleep, social life, financial security, celebrating birthdays, even life and limb (due to paper cuts from stuffing headshots and résumés into 9-by-12 envelopes for talent agency submissions). Others lose or gain weight for a role. Tom Hanks gained and lost weight multiple times for various movie roles. At the age of 57, he was diagnosed with type 2 diabetes, and doctors have speculated that his extreme weight fluctuations as he prepared for roles could have played a role in his diagnosis.

Come on. What other professions do people sacrifice like this for? Only actors. It's crazy, and it's why we are often seen as the opposite of people.

But these are the sacrifices in order to *get and keep* the job. Never do we assume we will sacrifice in order to never get the job in the first place.

Except for me.

I worked as the director of the children's ministry at our church for about seven years. My boss allowed me to audition for roles as long as they didn't interfere with my work at the church. Once while on staff, I auditioned for a commercial for a national gas station chain. I received a callback but was surprised to find out that the callback was the next day in Austin, which was four hours away. The trouble was I was taking my children's ministry staff and volunteer team to attend a children's ministry conference the next day as well. Several volunteers on my team had taken off work, and others had found babysitters. I mentally rolled over my options—I could leave halfway through the conference and ask my team to take notes for me while I headed to Austin. Or I could stay for the entire conference and miss the callback.

I wanted to go to this callback. But what would it communicate about how I valued my team and their time, if I, their leader, decided to leave? It would be best to stay, right? But who turns down a callback for a big commercial and the possibility of a large paycheck? That's like the opposite of people. Surely my staff would understand and would encourage me to go?

Deep down, I knew the right decision was to stay. But just in case, I wanted God to give me a clear answer. I fasted from coffee the next morning and asked God to tell me through His Word what He wanted me to do. I came to Proverbs 8 that speaks of the blessings of wisdom and how important it is to exercise it. As I read, God confirmed He wanted me to stay the length of the conference and forgo the callback.

I wasn't happy about the sacrifice, and neither was my agent, who thought I was crazy and, again, the opposite of people. But I knew I needed to obey.

In my opinion, our obedience is not just one way we evidence our faith, I think it's *the* evidence of our faith.

We don't just make God famous by our words and what we say but by the living out of our faith regardless of what it costs us. God asks for our obedience despite the sacrifice.

As believers, God is always asking us to obey Him in some way. Obedience could be defined as something we don't want to do that we know we should do and we decide to do. It is literally leaving behind self for the sake of God. Obedience is probably one of the strongest ways we can show our allegiance to Him. And dying to me means living for Him, which glorifies His name. But this is hard, isn't it? Maybe God is asking you to obey and walk boldly and differently at work when all you want to do is blend in. Maybe you're not married, and God is asking you to stay away from sex when everyone else is pushing you toward it. Maybe God is asking you to forgive *that* person, again.

He asks for our obedience despite the sacrifice. I discipline myself into obedience. Obedience shows our character, and it glorifies God. Theologian W. H. Griffith Thomas said, "Life is a succession of tests, for character is only possible through discipline."

God isn't interested in our comfort as much as He is our character. So He will allow things to happen to us—even bring situations before us—that cause us to lean more into and look more like Him. Will I respond in obedience despite the sacrifice?

God asked Abraham to do this. He asked Abraham to sacrifice his only son. God wanted to see if He was really everything to Abraham. Would he obey despite the sacrifice?

I remember reading the story of Abraham and Isaac prior to having kids and thinking, *It would be very difficult if God asked me to sacrifice my child.* But now after having kids, it would be unthinkable if God asked this of me.

In my opinion, this is one of the craziest and most difficult stories in the Bible.

✳ The Great Ask ✳

> *After these things God tested Abraham and said to him, "Abraham!" And he said, "Here I am." He said, "Take your son, your only son Isaac, whom you love, and go to the land of Moriah, and offer him there as a burnt offering on one of the mountains of which I shall tell you."*

—GENESIS 22:1–2

Abraham was to sacrifice his only son on a mountain in the land of Moriah—on these same mountains God would later appear to David who built an altar to the Lord there (2 Samuel 24:16–25). Solomon also built his temple here (2 Chronicles 3:1), and on this mountain, God the Father would sacrifice *His* only Son.

A typical dad asked to kill his son would argue. Refuse. Fight. But Abraham was not typical. He was a man of extreme faith. He didn't do any of these things.

> *Abraham rose early in the morning, saddled his donkey, and took two of his young men with him, and his son Isaac. And he cut the wood for the burnt offering and arose and went to the place of which God had told him.*

—GENESIS 22:3

Simply obeyed? Just like that? Yes.

Abraham remembered God's covenant, which promised that many generations would come from him. "And I will make of you a great nation" (Genesis 12:2).

Therefore Abraham knew his descendants would come through Isaac.

{ *And behold, the word of the L*ORD *came to him: . . . "your very own son shall be your heir." And he brought him outside and said, "Look toward heaven, and number the stars, if you are able to number them." Then he said to him, "So shall your offspring be." And he believed the L*ORD*, and he counted it to him as righteousness.* }

—GENESIS 15:4–6

Abraham, believing everything that God said would come to be, knew that if Isaac was to be the forever heir, if God was going to allow Isaac to die, then God would have to raise Isaac from the dead.

{ *By faith Abraham, when he was tested, offered up Isaac, and he who had received the promises was in the act of offering up his only son, of whom it was said, "Through Isaac shall your offspring be named." He considered that God was able even to raise him from the dead.* }

—HEBREWS 11:17–19

Abraham also proved he believed this when he said to the two men who accompanied them on their three-day journey to the mountains, "Stay here with the donkey; *I and the boy will* go over there and worship and *come again* to you" (Genesis 22:5, author's emphasis).

* Abraham's Obedience and Trust Convinced Isaac to Cooperate *

As Abraham placed the wood on his son to carry, he held the knife. Isaac, seeing all the pieces necessary for the sacrifice, noticed something was missing.

> *And Isaac said to his father Abraham . . . "Behold, the fire and the*
> *wood, but where is the lamb for a burnt offering?" Abraham said,*
> *"God will provide for himself the lamb for a burnt offering, my son."*
> *So they went both of them together. When they came to the place*
> *of which God had told him, Abraham built the altar there and laid*
> *the wood in order and bound Isaac his son and laid him on the*
> *altar, on top of the wood.*

— GENESIS 22:7–9

If Isaac was strong enough to carry the wood up to the place of the sacrifice, then he was probably strong enough to resist Abraham. He could have run away from the over 100-year-old man when he started to bind him. But he stayed. Just like Jesus stayed when He, being supernatural, could have disappeared off the Cross. Surely Isaac had seen God's unending faithfulness to his dad. Surely he had seen his father's relentless trust of God in times past. And surely his father's radical trust in God is what caused Isaac to now fully trust God and Abraham, even with his own life.

The intense story continues as this father concedes to God and shows Him the depth of his commitment.

> *Then Abraham reached out his hand and took the knife to*
> *slaughter his son. But the angel of the LORD called to him from*
> *heaven and said, "Abraham, Abraham!" And he said, "Here I am."*
> *He said, "Do not lay your hand on the boy or do anything to him,*
> *for now I know that you fear God, seeing you have not withheld*
> *your son, your only son, from me." And Abraham lifted up his eyes*
> *and looked, and behold, behind him was a ram, caught in a thicket*
> *by his horns. And Abraham went and took the ram and offered it*
> *up as a burnt offering instead of his son.*

— vv. 10–13

God provided a substitute sacrifice to die in place of Isaac. God repeats this at the Cross, but this time a human replaces the lamb.

God Blessed Abraham's Obedience

> And the angel of the LORD called to Abraham a second time from heaven and said, "By myself I have sworn, declares the LORD, because you have done this and have not withheld your son, your only son, I will surely bless you, and I will surely multiply your offspring as the stars of heaven and as the sand that is on the seashore. And your offspring shall possess the gate of his enemies, and in your offspring shall all the nations of the earth be blessed, because you have obeyed my voice.

—vv. 15–18

For the first and last time in Genesis, the Lord swears an oath in His own name guaranteeing His promise. "For when God made a promise to Abraham, since he had no one greater by whom to swear, he swore by himself, saying, 'Surely I will bless you and multiply you'" (Hebrews 6:13–14).

What a story!

God Still Blesses Obedience

I stayed at that children's ministry conference. I stayed mad, but I obeyed God. A few days later I received an email from my agent that I booked the job. I didn't even go to the callback, and 400 people auditioned for the role. I did everything the *opposite* of what you do to book a commercial. But I believe I booked the job because God wanted to bless my obedience.

Will God respond this way to each and every act of our obedience? I don't know. But when we receive blessings due to our obedience, we must give credit where credit is due. Because through blessing, God is letting us know our obedience is His great desire.

> *You shall be careful therefore to do as the* Lord *your God has commanded you. You shall not turn aside to the right hand or to the left. You shall walk in all the way that the* Lord *your God has commanded you, that you may live, and that it may go well with you, and that you may live long in the land that you shall possess.*

—DETERONOMY 5:32–33 *(author's emphasis)*

> *Oh that they had such a heart as this always, to fear me and to keep all my commandments, that it might go well with them and with their descendants forever!*

—v. 29 *(author's emphasis)*

Like God blessed Abraham for his obedience, we see in Scripture again and again that obedience often brings blessing. In Luke 5, Jesus asks Peter to let his nets down into the deep part of the lake to catch fish. Peter told Jesus he'd been fishing all day and caught nothing, but since Jesus asked, he would do it. And the Bible tells us that after Peter obeyed they caught so many fish their nets broke (vv. 1–11).

But the opposite is also true. Moses lost the blessing of going into Canaan when he disobeyed God's instructions (Numbers 20:7–12). And the Israelites who left Egypt didn't get to see the Promised Land because they too didn't obey God.

> *For the people of Israel walked forty years in the wilderness, until all the nation, the men of war who came out of Egypt, perished,* because they did not obey the voice of the Lord; *the* Lord *swore to them that he would not let them see the land that the* Lord *had sworn to their fathers to give to us, a land flowing with milk and honey.*

—JOSHUA 5:6 *(author's emphasis)*

Our Obedience Proves Our Love to Him

Our obedience shows God we care more for Him than we do for ourselves. "By this we know that we love the children of God, when we love God and obey his commandments. For this is the love of God, that we keep his commandments. And his commandments are not burdensome" (1 John 5:2–3). "You are my friends if you do what I command you" (John 15:14). And this brings Him fame and glory to His throne.

Not only do we prove our love to God, but our obedience also gives others the courage to trust God too. Just like it did for Isaac.

People may look at our choice to obey and say we are the "opposite of people." Will we obey despite the sacrifice of their opinions?

In what area of your life do you need to obey God? Are you willing to do it despite the sacrifice?

Obedience is extremely difficult, especially because it always seems easier to go our own way. But my happiness and comfort are not what I'm living for. I'm living to make God famous despite the sacrifice.

May we, like Abraham, obey God, trusting He has the power to bring back to life anything He's asking us to destroy. May we act in radical obedience despite the sacrifice, and may the fragrant aroma of our obedience bring glory to His name.

Questions to Consider:

» Write down a time that you obeyed God.

» Did you receive a blessing as a result? What was it?

» What is God asking you to obey Him with right now?

» Will you do it despite the sacrifice? What will this require of you?

» How might your obedience give someone the courage to trust God?

» Ask some people who love you to pray you will have the courage to obey.

19

Trust Fall

God's last act of faithfulness is not God's last act of faithfulness. —Jim Johnson, senior co-pastor of Preston Trail Community Church, Frisco, Texas

My high school theater teacher, Mr. Larry Cure, built our theater department on the motto, "Trust. Excellence. Tradition." Trust was a big part of our experience as theater students. This ideology taught me that if actors trust each other, we will deliver a more authentic performance as a company, and, most importantly, we will impact the experience for the theatergoer. One way we built trust was throwing our lives into the hands of each other by doing "trust falls." All the time. One person would stand on a desk on the elevated platform in Mr. Cure's theater classroom. Other times he or she would stand on the edge of the stage in the auditorium. Now, to his credit, Mr. Cure probably didn't see all the other crazy places from which we did trust falls. And if he did, he would've surely put a stop to it. No matter where we were, a group of actors stood beneath, ready to catch the trusting, falling, crazy person. The person would face away from the group and cross their arms over their chest so as not to hit anyone on the way down. And then he or she would fall backwards, completely trusting the group below to catch them. I can't remember anyone who was not caught. The first fall off the new location was always the scariest. But when my fellow thespians caught me time and time again, I knew I could rely on them.

Trust falls are a lot like our life with God. He has proven Himself over and over again, and we have evidence of His past faithfulness to catch us. But unlike a proven trust fall where actors fall carefree into the arms of those they depend on, we don't always trust God to catch us the next time He asks us to fall into His arms.

* The Fast *

My mama always said, "Whenever you need to make a decision, pray for God to give you Scripture you can stand on. If you rely only on your feelings, they will fail you. Feelings change like the wind, but God's Word never does." So when I come to a place in my life when I need God's direction, I try to remember her wisdom.

I've always known God put me on this planet to speak and communicate. I know this almost as much as I know that when I come out of my bedroom on Saturday mornings, I'll find my two sons playing video games.

For most of my adult life, I'd served on staff for churches that didn't have a position for me to do what I knew God purposed me to do. I worked hard and tried to glorify God in the center of my work, but I longed for the opportunity to *communicate* the goodness and fame of God.

In my midthirties, I felt a nudging to move away from church ministry and into full-time communicating. I wondered if maybe God had grabbed His "God-microphone" and said, "Lisa Lloyd, please come to the stage."

I felt like my boys waiting to come downstairs on Christmas morning. I asked God, "Are you ready? I'm ready. Is it time? Is it? Huh? Huh? Tell me noooooowwwww!"

So I asked Him to give me "Scripture I could stand on" to confirm or contradict what He wanted me to do.

I fasted as I sought God's answer. I didn't fast from food or coffee this time but from TV. Y'all, I didn't watch *Downton Abbey* for a month to prove I was superserious about showing God how much I wanted to hear from Him. I know, I know, utter sacrilege. One morning during this fast I read Acts 22. Paul talks about how he thrived on persecuting Jesus and killing Christians. He even held people's coats while they stoned Stephen to death (Acts 7:58). But one day on a road to Damascus, Paul heard the voice of Jesus. And the Lord transformed Paul forever. After God's white light of glory left Paul blind for three days, Paul's buddies had no choice but to lead him by the hand into Damascus. A devout Jew named Ananias restored his sight through God's power and told Paul he would be a witness to all men of what he had seen and heard.

Then in Acts 22:16, Ananias said to Paul, "And now why do you wait? Rise and be baptized." My eyes locked on this passage, and I felt the Lord say to me, "Yes, Lisa, why do *you* wait? Rise!"

Yet the firstborn, control-freak-planner in me needed more. *Whoa, whoa, whoa. Hold the reins, Cowboy. Leave my job just like that? You haven't told me what's next. I don't have anything planned. I haven't lined up another job. I have no speaking engagements on my calendar, no publisher knocking down my door to publish my book. And you want me to just up and leave? I don't think—*

Before I could finish, His whisper interrupted my disbelieving whine fest. God showed me that after Paul's time with Ananias, He didn't give Paul a road map for his next step either. Paul had to trust God. Acts tell us Paul went back to Jerusalem and prayed. As Paul prayed in the Temple, God showed him the next thing, and he obeyed.

I argued. "But that's easy for Paul. If I heard the voice of God, I would trust too." *But wait a minute . . .*

Equipped with an answer to prayer and Scripture to stand on, I had no reason to doubt the Lord. But I sensed the enemy say to me, "Lisa, are you sure that's what God said to you? Maybe you didn't hear God completely. And so that means you can't really hear God speak to you through Scripture. Though you want to be released, it's safer to stay put." I panicked. Immediately, I opened my Bible again to Acts 22 and asked God to give me—a self-proclaimed unbelieving mess—more confirmation. God led me to verse 10 when Paul says to Jesus in the middle of the road that day, "'What shall I do, Lord?' And the Lord said to me, 'Rise, and go into Damascus, and there you will be told all that is appointed for you to do'" (Acts 22:10). And there it was. Rise and go.

So I resigned from my job. Like a crazy person.

I didn't know where this decision would lead financially. Would we have to downsize our home? Sell a car? Build an even tighter budget? But I feared disobeying God—who had now told me twice what He wanted me to do—more than losing the security of a paycheck.

Sometimes God asks us to do ridiculous things. He asks us to trust Him with impossible situations with no discernible plan for deliverance.

Maybe, like me, He's asking you to leave your job. Maybe He's asking you to stay. Maybe He's asking you to stay in your marriage when all you want to do is go. Maybe He's asking you to trust Him with a new job your husband might have, but it will move you across town or even across the country. Maybe He's asked you to believe He will give you the baby you've tried for years to have but can't. Yet.

What if you and I trusted Him with radical faith? How might this change us? How might this usher peace into our hearts? What if we weren't consumed by the facts of our circumstances? What if we, in the center of our storm, stepped out of our boat and fully trusted God?

* Step Out of the Boat *

God asked Peter to do this seemingly foolish act and step out of his boat in the middle of a storm.

In Matthew 14, we read how Jesus fed the infamous 5,000. But the number 5,000 accounts for only the men present. With all the women and children, the total that attended the miracle dinner could have topped 20,000 people. After this, Jesus wanted to not only show His 12 disciples His glory but also challenge their trust in Him in the center of a storm.

Dinner had come and gone, and in Matthew 14:23, Jesus heads

up to a mountain to pray. He asks His disciples to get in their boat and go to the other side of the Sea of Galilee. I'm not sure why they call it a sea because it was more the size of a lake—about four to five miles across.

These were fisherman. Their boat was their second home—they knew how to maneuver it and ride the water. They quickly got halfway across the sea. But by the time it got dark, a storm assaulted their boat. This must have been a beast of a storm because they battled the storm until sometime between 3 and 6 a.m. The wind and waves were so treacherous they fought this thing for close to nine hours. *Yikes.*

No doubt the disciples felt exhausted and frightened for their lives when Jesus came sauntering up beside them—without a boat and on top of the water. The disciples freaked and thought He was a ghost. Makes plenty of sense to me. But Jesus said to them, "Take heart; it is I. Do not be afraid" (Matthew 14:27). Commentator R. T. France says about the phrase, "'Take heart' is an assurance for those who have good reason for fear. It does not indicate that the crisis is not real, but that in the presence of Jesus fear can be dismissed."

Peter gathered his courage and said to Jesus,

> *"Lord, if it is you, command me to come to you on the water." He said, "Come." So Peter got out of the boat and walked on the water and came to Jesus. But when he saw the wind, he was afraid, and beginning to sink he cried out, "Lord, save me."*

—MATTHEW 14:28–30

Jesus reached out His almighty hand and grabbed Peter and said to him, "O you of little faith, why did you doubt?" (Matthew 14:31).

The word doubt *used here means to be "divided in two" or to doubt/waver (in opinion) in the Greek.*

Peter sank because he saw the wind and the waves. He saw the lightning and heard the thunder. Maybe he even saw creatures swimming below him. He was surrounded by everything that said, "This storm just might end you today." He feared what could happen to him, what could happen to the *future* of him. He was consumed by the facts of his circumstances.

But here's what I find crazy. Peter had just seen Jesus feed 20,000 people with a little kid's dinner of five loaves and two fish. And they ended up with more leftovers than they had food to begin with. And right before the fish-and-loaves miracle, Peter had returned home from a journey with another disciple where God used them to cast out demons and heal the sick. Prior to *this*, Peter had watched Jesus perform miracle after flippin' miracle. So Jesus asked Peter a perfectly reasonable question, "Why do you doubt?"

Why do *you* doubt?

The question God asked Peter is the same question He asked me when I doubted Him about leaving my job. "Why do you doubt?"

If you're like me, you've seen God work over and over in your life. We've experienced God's faithfulness, and He's caught us in every trust fall. The outcome may not always turn out the way we planned, and our journey may have been tough to walk through, but, ultimately, we're glad it happened because of all the good things it led to. We send emails, and we call people, praising God's goodness about what He's brought us through. We post about His awesomeness on social media. And we stand on stages at churches and testify to what God has done.

The truth is, just like Peter, most of us have enough backstory with God that we don't have an excuse to allow worry, anxiety, and fear to cause us to doubt Him or His purposes for our lives. All too often I allow my worries about today to negate God's past faithfulness to me.

We may face the scariest situation of our lives. But if we look behind us, we will see that He got us from the boat to right here, and He's never let us drown. In fact, it's a miracle we're standing here at all.

God shows us we can trust Him each and every time. He shepherds us through the little things so that when the big storms come, we've seen His track record, and we trust Him.

* Parking Spots *

Whenever I'm with my kids and a prayer comes to my mind, I try to remember to speak it out loud. I do this so my kids can see my reliance on God to answer my prayers and learn that they too can trust Him with anything. When I need a parking spot in a crowded lot, you better believe I'm voicing it. When I'm alone in the car, God answers my "parking spot prayers" about 90 percent of the time. But when my kids are with me, He jumps it up to around 99.9 percent. And since kids are like sponges, absorbing everything they see us do and hear us say, whenever we enter a parking lot now, I'll hear one of them say, "Dear Jesus, please give mommy a parking spot by the front door." And *boom!* One will open up right in front of us. I believe God does this for my kids so that they will know they can call on Him.

One day Deuce lost a racecar and hadn't told me about it. A few days later, I was in the kitchen when I heard him shout from the living room, "No way!" I ran to see what catastrophe had occurred. There he was, holding up the lost, but now found, car. With amazement on his face and awe in his voice, he said, "Mom! I prayed God would help me find my car, and He did!"

Sometimes God proves Himself faithful in the small parking spot moments so we trust Him with the big racecar ones. It's in these times that we remember His past goodness to us, and we have the faith to step out and fall into His arms in the center of our storm.

The thing is, we tend to focus on the marriage in crisis, the prodigal child, the singleness, the loneliness, the sickness, the broken relationship, the infertility, the economy, and the house we can't sell. We focus on the storm instead of the God who controls the storm. The God who has *always* controlled the storm. Well, He's still in control. And He still has a purpose for your life.

* Yesterday, Today, and Tomorrow *

So how do we trust God in the center of our no-way-out? We *remember* that the God of our yesterday is still the God of our tomorrow.

When I begin to let go of my control over tomorrow—as if I had any control in the first place—and I begin to let God steer, I show Him that I radically trust Him.

Radical trust is opening up my hands and saying, "God, You are the God of my storm, You are the God of my marriage, You are the God of my job. You love my kids more than I do, You love my spouse more than I do, You love me more than I do . . . and that's pretty hard to do. You are the God of this struggle, You are the God of my impossible, and You, God, are in control. So I'm gonna trust You when life doesn't make sense and when I'm scared to death because You are the God of my yesterday, my today, and my tomorrow."

Do we toss in the towel and not do anything when the wind and the waves threaten to destroy our boat? Do we sit around and wait for life to happen? Heck, no. God wants us to do everything we can, but He calls us to *trust* Him with the outcome, remembering He loves us like no one else does and wants to use our struggle for His glory and fame. We don't have to live divided in two.

Here's what happens when we remember the God of our yesterday is the God of our tomorrow: a *peace* inhabits us. The Bible tells us this "peace of God . . . transcends all understanding" (Philippians 4:7 NIV). And like this verse says, this peace doesn't make much sense because our circumstance hasn't changed. The wind and the storm still rage around us. The only thing that's changed is our *response* to both.

Then people look at us funny. They look at the storm in our lives and say, "You should be freaked out right now." And we get to respond, "That's true. I should be. But God's gotten me from the boat to right here, and He's gonna get me from here to there." Doesn't mean there won't be a storm. Just means He's in control. I'm not in control of my storm, but I *am* in control of my sinking, how fast I sink, or whether I sink. And I'm not gonna sink anymore. My God is faithful.

And when we relinquish control, guess what happens to the image of God for those around us? He is made famous. Through us. He uses us—in our utter weakness, despair, and depravity—for His utmost purpose: to glorify His name.

People watch us and gather the courage to trust Him too. Imagine the next time your kids face a difficulty at school, and they remember your trust in Jesus and push through. Or the next time your husband fears for his job security, he remembers your faith and follows your lead. The next time your co-worker fears she won't be able to pay her mortgage, she remembers your radical faith and trusts God to provide.

And so as you repeatedly "trust fall" into the arms of God, you multiply the fame of Him to all who watch. May we say, "I'm gonna walk into my tomorrow, confident that the God of my yesterday is with me." And because of our radical trust, may we make God famous.

Questions to Consider:

» How are you most like Peter?

» What do you find difficult to relinquish control of and trust God with?

» Have you ever considered fasting about this issue and even asking God to give you Scripture you could stand on? What might you fast from? For how long?

» If you were to give your issue to God, what do you imagine could result?

» "If I were to fully trust God with this, I would make God famous to my . . ." (choose all that apply):

☼Husband

☼Friend/Boyfriend

☼Kid(s)

☼Fellow Employees

☼Mom or Dad

☼Other _____

» Would this person/people possibly trust God more because of your radical faith? If so, how?

» Pray God will help you to fall into His arms, trusting Him to catch you. And as you do so, may you make God famous.

For the Fame of His Name
Spoken Word

Do you ever think about the scene Christmas night so long, long ago?
Not the scene in Bethlehem. But in heaven as she stared down on earth below.
And knew what was about to take place,
In a stable that night would rescue the whole human race.

Then all the angels turned their heads to watch the Son step off His throne,
And walk toward His Father, knowing He'd soon be alone.

As Christ approached the Almighty, both their faces fell.
And as Mary labored, the Father whispered, "Go bring Me glory, My Son. Farewell."

Christ handed over His robe and His crown,
His holy glory, this He would drown,
For if any human were to see it, they would fall facedown,
Not able to stand. But this was not God's plan.

Instead God would send His Son, the King of kings and the Lord of lords,
To be born and live like one in poverty,
Reflecting the exact heart condition of you and me.

He would look like a man, live like a gypsy.

And we would scoff at Him, not listening to His plea,
That He's the only answer to a life lived eternally.

God was sending His Son to die,
And would watch Him be crucified.

And though I can't imagine sending my child into the hands of angry men,
The Father had an eternal perspective that kept Him steadfast to the end.

As labor pains increased, the final parting grew nearer.
And the tunnel from heaven to Bethlehem grew ever more clearer.

I know there are no tears in heaven,
But surely this once they made an exception.

As Christ put on a cloak of humanity ready to be birthed,
Mary gave one final push,
And Emmanuel, God with us, came to earth.

As He grew, people marveled that a boy seemed so connected,
To the heart of the Father, something no one expected.

And He grew. And He grew in wisdom and in stature,
And the favor of God and man was captured,
By a young boy who at age 12 was already a pastor.

His life confused the church leaders of the time.
He spoke against them because they thought sinners should pay for their crimes.
Leaders pushed aside the offenders, disgusted by their ways.
But Jesus responded differently, not with shame but with grace.

When the sinful woman came carrying a jar of expensive perfume,
The Pharisees stared accusingly and didn't give her room,

To reach the One who didn't see her sin.
All He needed was to be let in.

And she knew it too.
I know I need Him, and you and you.

A new woman, she left there with His name on her lips.
And God's plan was for her to share her rescue to the tips
Of the earth.

See the reason for her liberation and redemption,
Was not just for freedom, but so that she would lengthen,
The fame of His name.

Wouldn't you know we, sinful people too,
Share the same job of this woman? Yes, me, and yes, you.

Christ continued to confuse brother after brother.
That's because man thinks one thing but God thinks another.

Jews thought He was the Messiah, the prophesied one come home—
Born to redeem the people from the tyranny of Rome.
But Jesus came not to rescue one generation from their dreadful oppression,
But to rescue all nations from their sinful condition.

As He approached His final hours He didn't ride a glamorous horse fit for a king,
But the shameful Cross rode Him all the way to Calvary.

He had to die because blood had to be shed,
To rescue you and me from a life lived dead.

And He would do it again. And again.
But will He need to? No, never again!

Death done once. Blood shed for all,
Satan is crushed. Payback for the fall.

And the Son will again be sent back to the earth,
But not as baby ready to be birthed.
No, the clouds will roll back, and the Lord will descend,
As the Conquering King who has no end.

With a cry of command, the trumpet will sound,
Redemption complete. The lost are now found.
Satan defeated. And locked forever away.
We are brought home, oh, what a day!

So let's never forget the reason for the cradle,
And the reason for the tree,
Is the redemption of man and God's ultimate glory.

May we never live another minute the same.
May we forever live for the fame of His name.
In light of our own redemption story,
May our lives be our worship and to Him be the glory.

Written and originally performed by Lisa for the Women of Woodcreek Church, Richardson, Texas, 2014.

New Hope® Publishers is a division of WMU®, an international organization that challenges Christian believers to understand and be radically involved in God's mission. For more information about WMU, go to wmu.com. More information about New Hope books may be found at **NewHopePublishers.com**. New Hope books may be purchased at your local bookstore.

If you've been blessed by this book,
we would like to hear your story.
The publisher and author welcome
your comments and suggestions at:

newhopereader@wmu.org.

Use the QR reader on your smartphone
*to visit us online at **NewHopePublishers.com**.*